Praise for
Inclu

This practical book lays out 99 useful decisions you can make to help EDI take root and flourish in your organisation. The 100th is to buy it and start putting them into action.

Michael Bungay Stanier | Author of *The Coaching Habit*

Books on EDI often fall into the trap of being a bit academic, preachy or unrelatable. This is the opposite: practical, warm, accessible, and rich in specifically what to do and what not to do. And written for us by someone who's helped organisations large and small do this and flourish. As Catherine says, 'Everyone should be able to make their own cup of tea' — this step-by-step user guide will show you how.

Haider Imam | Partner | EY

Catherine has done an amazing job to cover a vast subject area so comprehensively and engagingly. It's full of practical and accessible insights backed up by evidence and illustrated with real life experiences. This is a book I look forward to dipping into whenever I need a dose of Catherine's properly authentic approach to make sure I'm not being complacent.

Jenni Allen | Content Director | Which?

Having worked with Catherine before, I knew I'd love reading her book! It's really accessible because she shares practical examples of what's worked, as well as what hasn't. And provides simple steps to educate and change culture by ensuring inclusion is led by every business area, not just the People team. I've experienced this in action, so I know it works. This book is a must read for anyone needing to embed inclusion into their business.

Lorna Kerr | Global HR Director | MediaCom

Wherever you are on your EDI journey, this indispensable and highly relatable guide is packed with all the ideas you need to deliver positive outcomes and change. Catherine's deep cross industry EDI experience combined with her unique ability to take complex ideas and translate them into simple, practical, everyday actions can now benefit a much wider audience.

Anne Sewell | CPO | dentsu international

Conscious Inclusion is such an important topic to support today's society. The book positions EDI as the human case rather than the business case and encourages you to operate to the notion of *'you don't have to solve the world problems, but you can do something'*. Individuals do not have to shoulder the full responsibility, but it's the sum of the small parts that's huge.

Phil Sampson | Global Procurement Director | PepsiCo

Catherine's guidance keeps things simple and focuses on outcomes. This book is packed full of stories and the practical decisions you can make, backed up with evidence for why it works. Reading it will inspire your progress and boost confidence in how to do it.

Ade Rawcliffe | Group Director of Diversity and Inclusion | ITV

Most of us wants to be inclusive, and most of us believe we are. However, both our genes and social upbringings gives us habits and biases that make us unconsciously exclude fellow human beings. In this much needed book, Catherine helps us become aware of our thinking and take action to change our behaviour and organisations from the inside and out.

Berit Lewis | Author of *Ageing Upwards: A mindfulness-based approach to the longevity revolution*

Catherine's book is completely consistent with her consultancy style; highly enjoyable, thought provoking and hugely practical. I'd like a copy for every one of my board, executive team, senior leaders and key influencers to guide our organisation in creating a fairer society. There's no preaching, or lecturing; just really useful contextual examples and key decisions that bring to life how to continue the equity and inclusion journey that we are all on.

Julie-Ann Haines | CEO | Principality Building Society

Conscious Inclusion is a brilliant book for anyone who is struggling to make their organisation more inclusive. It's inspiring but also supremely practical - giving a range of decisions to make that cover all the possible angles. The inclusion agenda can be daunting, but this book gives you real-life tools to make changes.

Lucy Adams | CEO | Disruptive HR

Catherine helps you easily glide from contemplating EDI to actually doing it, in some very quick and simple ways. If you're leading a team, department, or a whole organisation this book will help you do some genuine good in the world.

Jo Rackham | Director of Reward and Policy | John Lewis Partnership

Catherine's written an inclusion masterclass that feels like a great conversation. It's easy to read, quick to digest and thought-provoking in all the right places. It's also a veritable Smörgåsbord of practical tips, advice and actions brought to life through great stories - the sort of actions that anyone can immediately take into the workplace to make a real, positive difference.

Darren Towers | Group Head of Inclusion, Equity and Wellbeing | Spirax-Sarco Engineering plc

The real power of this book is its practicality. Catherine's warmth and experience gives leaders both the clarity and confidence to get started with EDI or supercharge their existing work for even greater impact. Read from cover to cover, or dipped in and out of, this book will help you build a more diverse, equal and inclusive organisation.

Louise Johnson |Former HR Director | Sky

This book is brilliant! I've highlighted many aha moments and written notes all over it. The content is accessible, inclusive, common sense and pragmatic. It is hugely relevant - sometimes poignant, sometimes humorous, and often challenging. And most importantly of all it will help change the world of work for the better, for everyone. I can't wait to pore over it again and I've bought copies for lots of other folk.

Sally Jones-Evans | Board Chair | Non-Executive Director | Trustee

Catherine has achieved something really difficult with this book being both comprehensive and highly practical. No stone is left unturned in her assessment and the world would be a better place if organisations did even 20% of what she suggests. Catherine's guidance also makes it easy to embrace the small changes if you're wondering where to start. This book will make a big difference to your leadership and your business.

Mark Allan | General Manager | Bupa Dental Care

Conscious Inclusion

How to 'do' EDI one decision
at a time

CATHERINE GARROD

First published in Great Britain by Practical Inspiration
Publishing, 2023

ISBN   9781788604284   (print)
       9781788604277   (epub)
       9781788604260   (mobi)

Want to bulk-buy copies of this book for your team and
colleagues? We can customise the content and co-
brand *Conscious Inclusion* to suit your business's needs.

Please email info@practicalinspiration.com for more
details.

Dedicated to

The Golds, for believing I can do anything,
for as long as I can remember.

And every changemaker that inspires me
and helps me learn.

Contents

Welcome to Conscious Inclusion

I'm so pleased you're here. I wanted to put something super practical into the world to support all the brilliant people advocating for change in their own organisations. Because I see so many people working really hard, and not always making the progress their effort deserves.

This book is packed full of stories and examples. And the guidance I'm giving you has been tried and tested in the multiple organisations I've had the pleasure of working for and with.

I've also had overwhelming support from people across industries and sectors who read the first draft. They gave me both critical and encouraging feedback, so that I could make the guidance even better. For that, I'll be forever grateful.

Here's some of what they said:

'Your approach to editing this book is a lovely example of how you practice inclusion in what you do. Thanks for including me'.

'It is so comprehensive. I was impressed by the sheer breadth. It went further than most books or papers I've read'.

'What I love most is that it comes across as approachable, easily digestible and deliciously practical'.

'This book is a very important contribution to its genre. One of the biggest USPs is its relatable, informal tone, that ensures readers are comfortable and feel like inclusion is "doable"'.

'The focus on action is important and something unique about this book'.

I hope you enjoy reading it too. Because I love to think about the collective impact of all of us leaving the world a little bit better than we found it.

Let's begin.

Part 1

Why is EDI so hard?

B efore we dig into what not to do and what to do instead, let's understand why the work of inclusion can be challenging and won't change overnight.

The language of inclusion often gets mixed up

I'd like to clarify what the acronym on the front cover of this book stands for. EDI: Equity, Diversity and Inclusion. You're likely to have heard many alternative acronyms, for example: D&I: Diversity and Inclusion, DIB: Diversity, Inclusion, Belonging, or JEDI: Justice, Equity, Diversity, Inclusion. There are many more, and it doesn't really matter which one you use, as the work itself should take centre stage.

Diversity, inclusion and belonging

These words often get used together and it's useful to separate them out for a shared understanding. I like to use the party analogy I first heard from Vernā Myers, VP of Inclusion Strategy at Netflix:

- **Diversity** is who is on the guestlist (fact)
- **Inclusion** is who gets invited to dance, versus standing round the edge feeling awkward (choice)
- **Belonging** is dancing like no one is watching, dancing to the music of your choice, or not dancing and no one gives you a hard time. It's also knowing you're really welcome (feeling)

Fairness

The initial illustration for the bicycle Equality and Equity graphic was created by the Robert Wood Johnson Foundation and it works brilliantly to illustrate what fairness is and isn't.[1]

Equality is treating everyone the same, which I often refer to as *'one-size-fits-all'*. In the first image four people are given identical bikes. The smallest person struggles to reach the pedals, the average-height person is cycling well, the tall person has their knees up by their chin and their back is hunched. And the person who uses a wheelchair can't use the bike at all.

Equity is giving people what they need to create the same opportunity. In the second image the smallest

> ❝ *Equity is giving people what they need to create the same opportunity.*

person has a smaller bike, the average height person keeps the average bike, the tall person has a larger bike. And the person who uses a wheelchair has a bike that can be pedalled with your hands. They can all now get from A to B.

LGBT+

Lesbian and **Gay** describe the attraction to people of the same sex, and **Bi** describes attraction to people of more than one sex.

Trans is an umbrella term for everyone whose gender identity (internal sense of self) is not the same as the sex they were assigned at birth. This can come with an overwhelming sense of unease and be an isolating and vulnerable experience.

- **Transgender** describes a person who may have surgical procedures or take hormone replacement therapy for their body to reflect their gender identity.
- **Non-binary** is a catch-all word for gender identities that are not exclusively feminine or masculine. Some people identify with both, some identify between, and some identify and present themselves as a woman or a man on different days.

± recognises the wide variety of terms used to describe sexual orientation and gender identity.

Some more language used when talking about people inside and outside the LGBT+ community includes:

- **Pronouns**, which are used to describe yourself or others. For example, *I, you, she, he, they.*
- **Cisgender**, which describes everyone who identifies with the sex they were assigned at birth.

Lived experience

Privilege. I love this quote shared on Instagram by Janaya Khan – *'Privilege isn't about what you've gone through, it's about what you haven't had to go through'*.

I've had some pretty hard life experiences. Who hasn't? I also recognise I have several privileges. One is being White and never being racially profiled as someone more likely to commit a crime. Another is having a body I can move without assistance, and not needing to do significant advance planning when travelling on public transport.

To reflect on your own privileges, look at the table and count how many aspects of your life fall into the most advantaged, some advantage and least advantaged columns:

	Most advantaged	Some advantage	Least advantaged
Disability	No disability	Limited mobility	Needs assistance to move around
Age	Adult	Young person	Senior
Body size	Slim	Average	Large
Skin colour	White	Can pass as White	Dark
Sexuality	Heterosexual	Can pass as heterosexual	Visibly LGBT+
Gender	Cisgender man	Cisgender woman	Visibly trans or non-binary
Language	English	English as a second language	Non-English speaking
Mental health	Robust	Mostly stable	Vulnerable
Neurodiversity	Typical brain	Some neurodivergence	Significant neurodiversity e.g., severe autism
Transport	Drives	Uses public transport	Little or no access
Housing	Owns property	Rents property	Homeless
Education	Higher education	College	School
Wealth	Rich	Comfortable	Poor

I have nine in the most advantaged column. Being aware of this helps me understand that in those respects, life is a lot easier for me than it is for someone who has the same nine in the least advantaged column.

This awareness helps make the work I do better and reminds me most of us have some kind of privilege.

Intersectionality describes the links between different forms of discrimination that can overlap. For example, a Black woman may experience both racism and sexism at the same time. Or a 58-year-old man using a wheelchair may experience both ageism and ableism at the same time. For these people their *'isms'* intersect in ways that significantly impact their lives.

Describing groups of people

When talking about the demographic groups of people in the workplace and wider world, the words often used are *'majority'* and *'minority'*, and these words work well to describe the population sizes.

However, when describing the demographic groups of a specific team, department, consumer base etc., I'd encourage you to use *'overrepresented'* and *'underrepresented'* instead:

Overrepresented describes the fact that there are more people with some characteristics than we'd expect based on the general population. For example, men make up 49% of the general population, but they make up a much higher proportion of leadership roles. So, men are overrepresented in those positions.

Underrepresented describes the opposite. For example, 25.6% of the population in England and Wales are an ethnicity other than White British, but they occupy a much lower proportion of leadership roles. So, they are underrepresented in those positions.

As you work to build an inclusive culture it's important to acknowledge people have unique experiences of discrimination. And addressing overrepresentation helps you ensure the whole of society is fairly represented in your organisation, and therefore that you remain relevant in the future.

We inherited a world that doesn't work for everyone

Why is EDI so hard? It's a question I get asked a lot and it's a good one as it's key to understanding the work involved. Chances are, if you've bought a copy of this book, you already have a good awareness, may be feeling a bit overwhelmed, and you're super practical and just want to know what to do.

Let me reassure you by saying that none of us will ever know everything. And that's ok. Even this book will need updating as our understanding of society and the different things we all need evolve.

Back to the question. It helps to learn how we got here, so let's take a look at a sample of events in UK history:

- **1760–1820/40** The industrial revolution separated work and families, resulting in men becoming the primary income provider and women becoming the primary care provider.[2] Before that families lived and worked together, providing a product or service to their community.

- Before **1918** no women were allowed to vote, compared to 58% of the male population. After 1918, the only women who could vote were those over the age of 30, who also had to meet a property qualification (read White and wealthy). This was in comparison to virtually all men over the age of 21, plus men in the armed forces from the age of 19. It wasn't until **1928**, less than a hundred years ago, that women and men had the same voting rights.[3]

- It's said we were influenced in **1926** to adopt the working hours of 9–5 from the routine and repetitive world of manufacturing cars.[4] The 24-hour clock was split into 3 x 8 hour shifts to maximise how many cars could be produced. The 9–5 shift has the daytime hours many of us are familiar with today, but that model wasn't designed for thinking time, creativity, or innovation. As that was all left to those in charge – also known as command and control.

- It was illegal to be gay just over 50 years ago, still is in many countries, until the Sexual Offences Act **1967** decriminalised sex between two men over 21 and '*in private*'.[5]

- Census data is published every 10 years and ethnicity in England and Wales was reported as 94% White as recently as **1991**.[6] The White population has decreased steadily to 91% in 2001, 86% in 2011 and 81.7% in 2021. This is since the British Government invited workers from abroad to support the reconstruction work after the Second World War, and the people who accepted that invitation now have multi-generational families.

- The Disability Discrimination Act only came in **1995** and it's not that far back in our history that people with disabilities were forcibly removed from families and put into mental institutions.[7]

- The Equality Act **2010** was introduced to consolidate previous discrimination acts. It covers nine protected characteristics to legally protect people from discrimination in the workplace and in wider society.

- **Today**'s workplace is typically better suited to neurotypical brains despite estimates suggesting 1 in 7 people are neurodiverse.[8] This refers to the different ways our brains process information; for example, people with autism or dyslexia are considered neurodiverse. The workplace is also usually better suited to extroverts, despite estimates that at least a third of people are introverts, who tend to need quieter spaces to recharge away from the hustle and bustle of an open-plan office.[9]

You might be thinking, so what?

Well, those in positions of power, for the longest time, were typically upper-class, heterosexual, White, able-bodied, neurotypical men. And they've designed the world based on what made sense to them. So, our laws, policies, research endeavours, services, workplaces, marketing, broadcast content, products... and everything in between, work better for you if you share that same demographic makeup. And less well if you don't.

Is it all their fault? Absolutely not.

But we must bust the myth of meritocracy which attributes success *purely* to hard work.[10] Yes, we can continue to acknowledge that people have worked hard and genuinely accomplished brilliant things. We must also acknowledge that the world is rigged in favour of people who share a similar profile to the people making decisions about how everything works.

The global population has increased from just over 1 billion to 8 billion in 200 years. That's a MASSIVE shift! And it means our demographics are ever-changing, so it's our collective responsibility to redesign it to work better for everyone. It's a big job for organisations that have been around for a while. And the days of providing a one-size-fits-all approach are rapidly expiring. Phew!

Consumers and employees are demanding a better experience

On 25 May 2020, as many of us were locked down during the global Covid-19 pandemic, the world witnessed White police officer Derek Chauvin kill George Floyd, a Black man who was pleading to be able to breathe. This particular act of inhumanity was caught on camera and the footage spread around the world. It sparked global outrage and people from every ethnic background took to social media, me included, to call for organisations to demonstrate they were against racism.

At the time, I was leading inclusion at Sky, Europe's leading media and entertainment company. I had just one person in my team and an awesome network of over 9,000 changemakers, across six employee networks, in a workforce of 24,000 collaborating to make Sky more inclusive. Our collective impact led Sky to be named Most Inclusive Employer in the UK 2019/2020[11] and 80% of the teams across Broadcast, Tech, Customer Service and Corporate Functions had increased their diversity since 2017.

I was regularly asked to share our approach outside Sky. And recognising that the same approach doesn't work everywhere and that different organisations would be at different stages, I set up a quarterly *'share and learn'* call for people from any organisation to take part in if they wanted to.

Each quarter I picked three topics and facilitated the swapping of failures, success stories and questions. We had leaders and passionate volunteers from Retail, Hospitality, Jewellers, Housing, Consumer Insights, Fast Moving Consumer Goods, Financial Services, Consulting, Utilities, Media and anyone else who was keen to influence their own workplace. It was a safe space for open discussion and we all learnt tons.

We had a call not long after George Floyd was killed and it was apparent everyone's organisation had underreacted, then overpanicked. Leaders had jumped to action, trying to solve systemic racism, without understanding the complexity of our history, the work involved or the impact on colleagues and consumers. You could feel how deflated everyone was.

I became the voice of optimism and said something like '*it's not going away this time, because consumers and employees from every ethnicity are speaking out and demanding more from who they work for, and who they spend their money with. It'll probably be bumpy for the next couple of years as the understanding about the reality of the work grows, and attention turns to creating sustainable change*'.

That was my catalyst for leaving Sky and setting up Compelling Culture. I wanted to work with multiple organisations and guide them to focus on the work that addresses root cause and actually makes a difference.

The scale of the task feels overwhelming

When I first joined Sky, my role was all about people involvement and it brought three areas of employee experience together: employee engagement, employee voice, and diversity and inclusion.

The bit I was most nervous about was diversity and inclusion. It felt like an enormous responsibility, and I was worried about being the expert for lived experiences I'd never had. I mean, how can anyone do that role when everyone's lives are so different?

I'd grown up with an internal sense that the world wasn't fair but didn't yet fully understand, or have the words to articulate that the world didn't work well for everyone and I didn't yet know what would be involved in making an organisation more inclusive.

Thankfully, I was hired for my ability to listen, challenge the status quo, and turn data insight into meaningful action. I was confident with engagement survey data and knew how to guide leaders to do the things that mattered most for their teams. I also had access to someone at every level in every department through the Sky Forum, which was a group of 100 employees elected by peers to represent their views. I had a track record for guiding organisations through culture change and collaborating to find the right approach. I realised the work of inclusion was no different.

About this book

I believe anyone at any level can play a part to make their team, department or whole organisation more inclusive. So, this book is written for the person with no line management responsibility, the network leader, the inclusion manager, the leader who wants to leave a legacy and every director, board member and trustee.

My guidance will make the seemingly intangible tangible, by breaking down complexity into simple actions that make the work already happening even better.

You'll see that this isn't purely about HR or the person with inclusion in their job title doing all the work. Instead, it's about how to build conscious inclusion into every decision made for colleagues, customers and the wider community.

Throughout my career, I'm grateful to have been surrounded by people who've challenged my thinking. And I've been empowered to experiment and fail fast, so I could find what works. I hope sharing what I've learnt will help you sprinkle some magic on the marvellous work you do.

Make this book yours

I would love you to make this book one you can refer to quickly. And will consider it a compliment if you fold the pages, underline stuff and scribble notes.

It took me years to ruin a new book and now I'm a total convert. Go for it.

If you can't bring yourself to ruin this book, you're listening to it, or you'd like to pass it on when you've finished, why not download the Conscious Inclusion workbook and make notes there. You can find it at www.compellingculture.co.uk/book

Reflection section

Key themes of Why is EDI so hard?

- There are many different acronyms, and it doesn't really matter which one you use as it's the work itself that should take centre stage.

- Those in positions of power for the longest time designed the world based on what made sense to them.

- No one can be the expert for every lived experience.

Part 2

What are the traps to avoid?

I consider myself optimistic, so writing a whole section focused on what not to do feels uncomfortable. I had a little word with myself and wrote it anyway as there is so much noise that distracts organisations from doing what's needed.

Here goes.

Fear, blame, compliance and insincerity

The fear of getting it wrong

Fear is something that comes up in every conversation with new clients, no matter how much progress they've made so far. And that's because we're much more aware that some of the language and beliefs we consumed growing up are likely to be out of date today. So, everyone is worried about saying or doing the wrong thing, and for leaders, the fear is being exposed as someone who doesn't have the answers. And this can feel scary.

The truth is that none of us will ever be fully confident, as we've each only lived our own lives and there's 8 billion people on the planet.

A healthcare client told me they'd be fully confident when they could answer every product and service query related to the diverse needs of their millions of consumers. I encouraged them to aim for (an ambitious) 80% as their offering would be constantly evolving and

> **" The truth is that none of us will ever be fully confident, as we've each only lived our own lives and there's 8 billion people on the planet.**

every person's needs will be specific to them. I noticed the tension in their shoulders drop immediately.

Another client told me they weren't ready to fully embrace inclusion work yet, as they needed to build more confidence first. While timing is everything, waiting for a perfect set of conditions (there's no such thing, by the way) to create change typically means you get left behind. And if the whole world did that, we'd never make any progress.

Fear is a good driver. It means people understand the sensitivities involved, care about the people they're surrounded by, and want to avoid getting it wrong. It also makes people more receptive to investing time and effort into finding the right approach. So, it's good to acknowledge those fears and embrace any discomfort, because that discomfort is telling you something isn't right. And that's a powerful place to learn.

Deliberately making people feel uncomfortable

There's a fine line between holding space for people to reflect on topics that are uncomfortable, and deliberately making people feel uncomfortable.

Providing a list of things that aren't good enough, and telling people they should know better, rarely motivates change. Particularly if that list is challenging long-held views or requires ripping up a process without knowing what the alternative is.

I'm often asked how to '*deal with*' people who speak up against inclusion. I'd encourage you to listen and find out what there is to learn. Maybe your commitment to inclusion feels like it doesn't include them. Maybe they feel like no one cares about their experiences. Everyone wants to be heard and it's essential to hear all perspectives. When we fall into, '*I'm right, you're wrong*', both sides lose. Just look at UK and US politics. We all need to become much more tolerant of each other's views, especially when we don't agree. Being more curious will help you identify the absolute differences and surface the commonalities to build from.

> **"** *When we fall into, 'I'm right, you're wrong', both sides lose.*

If people are being deliberately harmful, your organisation will have policies in place to handle that.

Another regular question I'm asked is, '*How do I influence the people who aren't yet interested?*', as there's often real frustration that people don't care or understand. Now this may be surprising – my advice is to redirect your energy and focus on boosting the people who do get it, are agitating for change and making an impact. Highlighting what your changemakers are doing will inspire more people to get involved and that's how you build momentum for creating lasting change across an organisation.

Mandatory unconscious bias training

Don't get me wrong, learning about our biases and how to consciously include people is something I'm a BIG fan of (maybe the title of the book gave that away). It's making that sort of training mandatory that I'd discourage you from pursuing.

At best, mandatory unconscious bias training makes the people who care about inclusion feel good that the organisation is making this investment. Many people will be interested at the time but won't remember the key learning points two weeks later when they're under pressure. And at worst, the people who aren't particularly motivated now have a reason to be defiant about any less desirable behaviour – *it's my unconscious bias, I can't help it.*

My favourite research on this is highlighted in a Harvard Business Review (HBR) article by Frank Dobbin and Alexandra Kalev – *Why Diversity Programmes Fail.*[1] In it, they write:

> 'Firms have long relied on diversity training to reduce bias on the job...Yet laboratory studies show that this kind of force-feeding can activate bias rather than stamp it out. As social scientists have found... companies get better results when they ease up on the control tactics. It's more effective to engage managers in solving the problem'.

So why do so many organisations keep doing it?

Your lawyers may tell you that you need to demonstrate what percentage of people have completed mandatory unconscious bias training. This is in case you're required to defend a sexual harassment, racism, homophobic, or any other awful case, in a tribunal. A high percentage of people having done the training is used to argue that the organisation can't be held responsible for an individual's behaviour.

Other influences are external EDI benchmarks that sometimes award extra points for high percentages of people having been through mandatory training. The suggestion here is that the more people who have completed mandatory training, the more committed the organisation is.

As a side point - if every manager went on every training programme a benchmark or awards programme recommended, they'd never spend any time with their teams.

There are better ways to demonstrate organisational commitment and this book will give you lots of advice about what, and how, to do it.

You can offer unconscious bias training as part of a

> " *You can offer unconscious bias training as part of a wider plan, but don't make it mandatory, because compliance doesn't change behaviour.*

wider plan, but don't make it mandatory, because compliance doesn't change behaviour.

The worst behaviours are ignored

You can't be committed to inclusion and at the same time let problematic behaviours go unchallenged. It just doesn't work, as people won't believe you're committed to creating a better environment when they experience people getting away with harmful behaviour.

Banter
If banter about ageism, ableism, homophobia etc. is part of regular conversation, and people who don't participate in it are excluded for having a 'sense of humour bypass', that's not an inclusive environment. And it's likely the people who aren't part of the largest 'norm' group are hiding parts of themselves for fear of being ridiculed or treated as 'other'. Or they are avoiding certain teams.

Whenever this comes up, it's clear there are repeat offenders, everyone knows who they are, and people assume they need to tolerate it because it happens so frequently.

Even when you think there's no one around who fits the target identity of the banter, don't forget, people have friends, family, and neighbours, so that meme that's being circulated could be mocking someone they care about.

Bullies

How about the people who micromanage, limit career development, exclude people from meetings or social events, display outbursts of rage in meetings, or constantly belittle others? They might appear to be incredibly charming and good at managing relationships with senior people, yet they're making their team, or the experience of some of the people in their team, miserable. This behaviour is toxic and the very opposite of inclusive. It must be dealt with swiftly and stopped.

The time we spend at work can be a big chunk of our lives, and people need to feel safe and valued. If you've invested in creating a set of values, use them as your foundation to respond when people behave inappropriately.

Predators

Then there's the person who always gets a bit handsy at the team drinks, stares too long at colleagues or suggests they go somewhere a bit quieter.

But Pervy McPerve brings in lots of money, so the leaders of the organisation pretend not to notice, and a *'let's all remember to treat each other with respect'* email goes out in advance of events.

This signals that the organisation is ok with sexual predators, and victims must protect themselves. Imagine the number of victims who've had to adjust their routines to stay out of danger.

And for the victims who find the courage to report, consider how many cases result in a settlement agreement for Pervy McPerve to leave with cash in exchange for silence. They move onto a new organisation and a whole new group of potential victims. Or the victim is silenced and paid off, and Pervy McPerve stays put, with an increased sense of predatory power.

Harvey Weinstein, anyone?

You need to send a clear message
Every woman I know has experienced predatory behaviour at work, on the streets or at home.

My most recent experience was this year, when small talk with a delivery worker rapidly escalated to sexual harassment. On the first occasion he stopped to

> *Every woman I know has experienced predatory behaviour at work, on the streets or at home.*

say hello when I was washing the car, and once he'd established I was a single woman, started saying things like *'I'm a randy old man'*, *'I'm too old for all that now'* and *'I should be so lucky'*. I was shocked and immediately disengaged from the conversation. The next time I saw him, I was wearing shorts and he was delivering a parcel. As he took a picture to confirm the delivery he said, '*ooh look at those legs, I'll be keeping that one*', and showed me the handheld device with a big grin on his face.

I was shaken by the violation and reported him to his employer. Long story short, they handled it terribly. Each time they offered reassurance he wouldn't be delivering in my area anymore, he turned up on my street, which left me putting trousers on every time I had to answer the door. I escalated it to his employer three times and ultimately reported him to the police. At the time of writing, they plan to invite him in for an interview under caution, because his employer's lack of action was sending a clear message – *you carry on, lads, and when victims speak up, we'll ignore them.*

That company delivers to every address in the UK, employs thousands of people and failed to act. I can only imagine how awful it would be working there, when there's such little regard for women's safety.

It's not enough to write words into a policy, you need to act, and fast. Especially if you're claiming to be committed to inclusion.

If these things are happening in your workplace, and you change it, this is how even the worst events can end up being transformative.

> " *Even the worst events can end up being transformative.*

Accountability in the wrong place

Lack of sponsorship

When people across the organisation are trying to make a difference but leaders aren't involved, this demonstrates a worrying lack of sponsorship. And it usually means progress will be limited.

Pressure on willing amateurs

There are often large numbers of employees willing their organisations to do better, highlighting the barriers that have long been in their way and providing tons of suggestions. These are incredibly valuable people to learn from and they often self-organise into Networks, Employee Resource Groups, Steering Groups, Committees etc. However, they usually have limited experience of taking an organisation through culture change, but because those people have *lived* experience, are vocal and passionate, it can get left to them to '*do the work*'.

Look different, be the same

The absolute worst case is when someone is appointed because they 'look' diverse, but the organisation wants them to operate like everyone else, prioritise comfort and ultimately do as they're told. And when the organisation fails to make progress, that person is blamed for not being good enough. And some will then conclude that 'diverse' people are not high performers. This one makes my blood boil.

Computer says no
The pain and frustration people feel when forced to use technology that doesn't adequately account for their needs can be so far removed from the minds of the people making decisions about tech investments and upgrades. This allows tech teams to get away with dismissing accessibility as too hard, too expensive, not being on the roadmap for this year, and not investing in anything that doesn't benefit the majority of their users. Ouch! Thankfully, times are changing.

Do more with less
When agreeing budget for anything to do with people, the goal is often 'efficiency' or do more with less. When you want to take an organisation through cultural change and redevelop systems and processes to work well for everyone, you need budget.

I just love this visual!

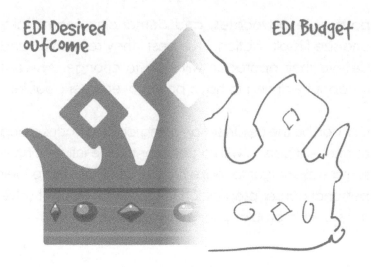

EDI Desired outcome

EDI Budget

To make your organisation inclusive, the people in senior positions with the power to influence change need to hold themselves accountable. Because a lack of leadership accountability leads to fatigue, sets everyone up to fail and risks reputational damage.

Empire building

Empire building is about amassing resources (people), budgets, management attention etc. into one place and gaining power. When it comes to inclusion (and many other things), it does more harm than good, because no one person or team can make an organisation more inclusive.

Ego gets in the way

This can look like someone suggesting they're the only person that understands inclusion, disengaging passionate advocates, and demanding teams take one-size-fits-all action. At best they're naïve and believe their approach will lead to change. At worst it's about wanting to have power over other people.

Or it can be the organisation being led by a 'focus group of one' – a person with a confident voice influencing a senior stakeholder to make big decisions that serve their personal career progression interests. But doesn't solve the systemic problems for everyone else.

Inclusion becomes exclusive

Employee networks dedicated to different areas of inclusion e.g., women, mental health, disability, can become so focused on hosting the biggest events and getting the most members, they end up competing with each other.

People and teams need to be delivering against one prioritised plan, with the autonomy and flexibility to deliver in their own way.

Think building bridges, not walls.

All expectation is on HR

All too often, the organisation is committed to change, but the only people expected to do anything differently is HR. There's a belief that if HR update the policies and recruiters provide a diverse shortlist, everything will be sorted.

If only it were that simple.

It's the decisions people make every day that make an organisation inclusive. Who gets invited onto projects? Who gets the annual recognition awards? Who gets put on stage at an industry event? Which customers are asked for feedback? Who's involved in research and product development? Which suppliers do you work with? And on and on and on.

It's really easy to sign up to the idea of your organisation being more inclusive. It's harder to change your own ingrained ways of doing things without clear direction.

My clients are mostly Chief People Officers and Chief Executive Officers who turn to me when they've made a good start and want to be confident they're investing their energy in the right places. I use a diagnostic tool that covers Employee Life Cycle, Customer, Buildings, Technology, and Wider World Impact. People from every level and department get involved to help me learn about what they do and how they do it. Once the

> "It's really easy to sign up to the idea of your organisation being more inclusive. It's harder to change your own ingrained ways of doing things without clear direction.

initial findings are validated, we co-create an inclusion strategy and roadmap that makes sense of the work they're already doing and makes it more inclusive.

Becoming an inclusive organisation extends far beyond HR.

The illusion of inclusion

Anonymised CVs

This is a 'fix' promoted as eliminating bias from shortlisting candidates for interview. It means stripping a CV of any personal characteristics e.g., age, race or gender, and some go a step further and remove education indicators.

Eye-opening studies have revealed that applicants changing their names to more English-sounding names boosts their chances of being selected for an interview.[2] Research carried out by academics at Oxford University found British citizens with names that indicate an ethnic minority background (including White ethnic minorities) have to send, on average, 60% more job applications to get a positive response from employers, compared to those with traditionally White names.[3] The researchers sent almost 3,200 fictitious applications and 24% of applicants of White British origin received a positive response from employers, compared with 15% of British minority ethnic applicants applying with identical CVs and cover letters.

The idea of anonymising CVs is often linked to the reported success of hiring more women into an orchestra. The musicians were required to audition behind a screen, so that selection decisions were made purely on musical ability.

When replicated in business, a manager reviewing a pile of anonymised CVs can only select a shortlist for interview based on skill and experience. Sounds good... but the replication is wonky because a musical audition provides an absolute example of the necessary skill, but a CV is a piece of paper that captures examples, and some people capture their experiences better than others. It's also wonky because there's no evidence that it works. And it's a highly manual process to remove details, so that time and effort could be better used elsewhere.

If you want your hiring to be inclusive, you can't place all responsibility on the process and hope it works. Instead, you need to equip recruiters and hiring managers with guidelines to make more inclusive decisions, so that they're aware of the tendency to shortlist and hire people similar to themselves and can actively work to overcome that bias.

> " If you want your hiring to be inclusive, you can't place all responsibility on the process and hope it works.

Programmes to 'fix' the underrepresented

Sending 'diverse' people on development programmes is often a central pillar in an organisation's efforts to become more inclusive. On the surface it feels good and looks like the organisation is doing something. But if the overrepresented people aren't being guided to do anything differently, the people who've been sent on those programmes continue working in the same environment. And it's that environment, not their personal attributes, that has been disadvantaging them all along.

Setting up programmes to help the people who 'haven't yet made it' (read women and minority groups) implies there is something wrong with them and they need help to be better.

It's not the case.

A study by Stephen Turban, Laura Freeman and Ben Waber showed women and men are treated differently at work.[4] They found that men got promoted more than women not because of difference in their own behaviour, but due to differences in how they were treated. Women had the same number of contacts as men, they spent as much time with senior leadership, they had indistinguishable work patterns, and they scored equally well in performance evaluations. Yet women in their study weren't advancing, and men were.

I was nominated for a 'Women in Leadership' programme early on in my HR career and was supposed to be delighted my potential had been recognised. Instead, I wondered why men weren't being sent on a programme to make fairer hiring decisions. In the first session, the chosen women were told to wear darker colours, lower the tone of their voice, speak more slowly and take up more space in meeting rooms. Essentially, we were being told to behave more like men.

I kid you not. I left the programme.

Instead of trying to fix the people who are absolutely NOT broken, we need to fix the environment, so everyone has the opportunity to grow their careers if they want to.

People are 'busy being busy'

More often than not, I speak to organisations that are hugely committed and have spreadsheets full of activity that's being tracked. Sounds ok, but the reality is they're trying lots of things at once, hoping some of it works, but no one knows for sure. This is a bit like using burst mode on a camera to take multiple pictures per second, and hoping one or two of your pictures look like a professional photographer took them. It rarely works.

❝ *Activity without measures of success is just people 'busy being busy' and creates an illusion of inclusion.*

Typically, ideas have been generated by asking employees, attending conferences, reading thought-provoking posts on LinkedIn, or trying things that have worked in other organisations. And all that's more than ok, if it aligns to a plan with measures of success. But usually that's not the case.

Activity without measures of success is just people 'busy being busy' and creates an illusion of inclusion. That illusion is obvious when annual reports highlight programmes, initiatives and activity, without the all-important evidence of impact.

Lots of activity is a good problem to have, because when you prioritise it and build it into a clear plan, you provide a path for people to follow. And as you start seeing progress, it inspires more people to do more.

Reflection section

Key themes of the traps to avoid

- Letting the fear stop you from getting started.

- Challenging someone's long-held views by telling them they should know better.

- Believing mandatory training will change your culture.

- Ignoring harmful behaviour.

- Leaving the work to people who hold no power.

- Believing one person or team can make your organisation inclusive.

- Expecting HR to make it all happen.

- Removing responsibility for hiring diverse teams from hiring managers.

- Focusing on fixing people instead of fixing the environment.

- Doing lots of activity without a plan and measures of success.

Part 3

How to create an inclusive culture

N ow for the good stuff. Hooray.

The goal for today, tomorrow, and the rest of your working, community and family life is Conscious Inclusion. So far, we've seen that much of the world we've inherited just

" Unless you're consciously including people, you're almost certainly unconsciously excluding people.

doesn't work as well for everyone. And that quick fixes, initiatives and programmes can often distract from getting on with the work that creates sustainable change.

Part 3 is about how you lead yourself and others. Making deliberately inclusive decisions is a massive part of the work that's needed. And I have the following text as a screensaver to remind me – **Unless you're consciously including people, you're almost certainly unconsciously excluding people.** Am I perfect? No. Am I a work in progress continuing to learn? Absolutely.

When we were drafting the inclusion vision at Sky back in 2017, the workforce was 65% male and predominantly White. I was hyper aware that increasing our focus on better including underrepresented populations might be perceived as excluding those who are overrepresented. As part of our research, we asked the Sky forum (a mixed population of 100 employees from every department) what inclusion meant to them. I'll always remember the feedback. It wasn't about being Black, Brown, lesbian, disabled, autistic etc., as those things were just expected. It was about no matter how long someone had been at Sky, whether they were frontline customer facing, leading the tech team, or working in live broadcast, they wanted to be valued for their contribution and their voice to count when they spoke up. And... they didn't want to hear about the business case, because that made it feel like it was all about money, instead of people. That feedback still inspires my thinking and has held true in every organisation I've worked with since.

Embedding inclusion into an organisation means going beyond the business case. It's about making inclusion meaningful for everyone and applying it to the work they do and the environment they're in.

<u>The decisions you can make</u>
The following chapters each have numbered decisions you can make to create a more inclusive organisation. You'll probably find you're already doing some of them and there's plenty more you can easily do. Others might need a longer-term investment. At the end of each chapter, I'll summarise the key decision themes and share some questions for you to reflect on. Parts 4–6 will follow this same approach, then when we get to Part 7, I'll help you prioritise what you'll do in the next 12 months.

Let's go.

Build solid foundations

Decision 1:
Use a model for change

You'll get results by building a shared plan people can see the value in and inviting them to get involved in their own way. Individuals and departments will move through four phases of inclusion maturity, and you can use these phases to lead the culture change.

Phase 1: Motivate

In all the culture change work I've been involved in, there are always good people, doing good work already, and one of my mottos is to start with what you've got and where you are now. Because you're never starting from zero. So, the first phase is to do internal and external research to uncover what's already happening. You'll need to gather data, understand regulator or investor expectation and listen to employee feedback. This provides the opportunity to meet new and existing demands and motivate both head and heart. On that point, it doesn't matter whether people are motivated by head or heart, because they both lead to the same outcome.

Once you've understood where you are today and what you need to do, bring people together to share what you've discovered, find out what resonates most, then prioritise what to do in the next 12 months. This process helps determine who will be involved and the level of investment needed.

To build a plan everyone can get behind, I recommend developing a shared overall ambition, with specific focus areas by department. For example, Tech could focus on addressing the underrepresentation of women to close the gender pay gap, Facil-

> " *To create the movement that is culture change, do one thing brilliantly until it sticks, then the next, then the next, then the next…*

ities on making buildings neurodivergent friendly, Sales on addressing the overrepresentation of White people in senior roles etc. etc. The fewer priorities a department has the better because progress comes faster with focus. To create the movement that is culture change, do one thing brilliantly until it sticks, then the next, then the next, then the next…

Whatever you choose to do, make sure you can measure it. You'll find out how in Part 4.

Phase 2: Activate
Once you've got your plan refined, help employees see how it's relevant to the work they do. People like to be part of something bigger than themselves and relating your overall ambition to their work is a great way to generate long-lasting results.

Then get on and deliver. I encourage you to experiment, test, learn and scale. Sometimes the best outcomes start with a pilot group of just five people. Find those early disruptors and start there.

As you make progress, there'll be a series of tipping points and momentum will pick up pace. It's awesome when you start seeing the ripple effect. Be patient, though, as it can take up to six months.

Clients typically stay focused in the activate phase for at least 12 months.

Phase 3: Accelerate

This is when you press pause to calibrate the plan. Add up all the successes you've had so far, redirect energy away from anything that hasn't really worked, and prioritise your actions for the next 12 months.

Phase 4: Lead

Once you're confident about your approach, share it with other departments, or across your industry or sector, so they can make progress too.

Decision 2: Create the belief change is possible

Most of the success in taking an organisation through a significant shift comes down to creating the belief it's possible. And you'll be off to a good start if you've involved people in defining and refining the ambition.

You want to build confidence and inspire people to get involved, and providing regular updates is a great way to do this. Think about listening to a heartbeat – what you want to hear is a steady rhythm, and your communication should be the same. It's reassuring, and when people can see progress happening, they really start to believe more is possible.

> " *Think of your communication as a lighthouse sending out a beam so bright, everyone can find their way, no matter how far away they are.*

It's a good idea to plug mini updates into the communications channels that are already used, and it's ok if this looks different in different departments.

When people hear about something regularly, it sends a signal this is something the organisation really cares about. If you have eight communication channels, use them all, as the goal is repeat, repeat, repeat for familiarity.

Think of your communication as a lighthouse sending out a beam so bright, everyone can find their way, no matter how far away they are.

Use a consistent message structure
Your communication should be kept as simple as possible. To shape your message, consider the one thing you want people to remember, along with what you'd like people to know, feel and do.

The message structure for this book is:

- **Headline message:** Conscious inclusion is making what you already do work well for everyone.
- I want readers to
    - **Know:** people in every team can make a difference.
    - **Feel:** hopeful, brave and energised.
    - **Do:** one thing brilliantly at a time.

For your organisation, every written or verbal message should bring your *headline* and *know, feel, do* answers to life. You can encourage people to deliver the sentiment in their own way rather than sticking to a rigid script. The aim is to remind people about the commitment to inclusion and provide opportunities for people to learn and get involved.

I encourage you to be transparent about any areas you're struggling to make progress with. This helps people see your commitment is authentic.

You should also communicate every small win and credit the people involved. This reinforces the fact that inclusion isn't down to one person or team and highlights work being done by people right across the organisation.

It might take a while to get the rhythm going, so be patient. You'll know it's working when people tell you how much they enjoy hearing about all the great progress.

Decision 3:
Have a plan for not always getting it right

A memory that sticks in my mind is when a group of colleagues approached me to develop support materials for people going through menopause. My initial reaction was to wonder if it was really an issue. I can't quite believe I'm saying that now, given the rise in awareness on TV and in the workplace over the last few years.

I attribute my reservation to being in my early 30s, having tons of female friends, working in a department full of women, and no one talking about it. I'm wiser now and realise that's much more to do with stigma, than there not being a real need for support.

Luckily my work has taught me to look for multiple sources of information, so I put some calls into Occupational Health and the legal department, and quickly realised menopause was in fact an area that needed attention. We got on with developing the materials.

> *You're human and won't always get it right, so it's good to develop a curious and collaborative approach, as this will significantly reduce the risk of getting it wrong.*

Thankfully there were employee networks who were further ahead in their thinking and bridged the gap by providing handy resources and links to external organisations.

You're human and won't always get it right, so it's good to develop a curious and collaborative approach, as this will significantly reduce the risk of getting it wrong.

Decision 4:
Set your inclusion leaders up for success

Inclusion is a broad and relatively new skill set in the workplace, and like any role, people come to it with varying levels of experience. Whether inclusion is someone's full-time role, 10% of their role, they're leading a network, or they've been doing this work for years, they need both private and public support.

Support might look like being given the autonomy to make certain decisions, regular coaching, time to do the work, or budget to seek external expertise.

Skills in strategy development, stakeholder relationships, collaboration and reflection are all great ingredients for an influential leader. Being able to flip between high-level ambition and detailed actions is another advantage. As well as the use of storytelling and being able to inspire a new way of looking at things.

A core part of this person's impact is to connect dots both internally and externally, and tie objectives to organisation purpose. When I was leading on inclusion at Sky, someone one described me as a conductor, as I didn't play the instruments; instead I directed those who did, just like in an orchestra.

I'm neutral about which part of the business inclusion teams or leaders report into, so long as they understand HR is one of their biggest stakeholders. As HR is where all the levers are for employee experience, including policy, process, recruitment and career development. And the HR team know which levers to pull when, to make the whole operation work.

If you're thinking of creating a new position, appointing someone internally who is trusted and well networked is often a good move. Provide them with external consultancy support and your organisation will go further faster than if you hired someone new and waited for them to settle in. I'm also a big fan of internal mobility and creating roles to develop and retain the talent you've already got.

Reflection section

Key decision themes

- People will move through change at their own pace.

- Regular communication is reassuring and inspires further action.

- Seek multiple sources of information to get things right.

- Inclusion leaders need to be supported.

Questions to answer before we move on

- What resonated most?

- What did you recognise that you're already doing?

- What did you learn?

Lead with courage and vulnerability

American professor, lecturer, author and podcast host Brené Brown is known for her research on shame, vulnerability and leadership. And I love how she talks about courage and vulnerability being the same thing. One of my favourite quotes from her work is *'I'm here to get it right, not be right'*.

> *'I'm here to get it right, not be right'.*
> Brené Brown

This is a helpful mindset to adopt for the work of inclusion. When you get it wrong, you can apologise, and people will forgive you when it's clear your intentions are good.

Decision 5:
Dedicate time to learn and share fears

Holding space to reflect and share vulnerability is an investment worth making. The topic of inclusion can be confronting if you've worked hard throughout your career and are now wondering if you've had advantages simply because of the skin colour, sexual orientation, wealth etc. you were born with.

Learning for Executive and Board teams
The collective courage of leadership teams tends to vary by industry and sector. I notice leaders at

organisations with a social purpose typically have a greater awareness of the inequities that exist across society.

Something many organisations share is the absence of an organisation-wide inclusion strategy that goes beyond describing initiatives. Another is the absence of leaders at the top who are already comfortable talking about inclusion. This combination can generate resistance to change in the early days, because these conversations are not always easy. If they were, boardrooms, workplaces, products and services would already be reflecting the diversity of people in our communities and nations.

It helps to know that understanding inclusion, and where it's missing, can be done one conversation at a time. And it's worth noting that when it comes to discussing people and culture, opinions can be free flowing and based on emotional responses and personal experiences, when compared to discussions about operations or numbers. That's to be expected and it would feel a bit odd if that wasn't the case. After all, we're all people, and this work affects all of us. So don't worry too much if there's a bit of tension at first.

> " *It helps to know that understanding inclusion, and where it's missing, can be done one conversation at a time.*

When presenting an inclusion strategy and roadmap to the Board at one of my clients, one of the directors told me and the Chief People Officer (CPO) that a discussion sharing the research, strategy and action plan, without the precise date the organisation would become inclusive, was a complete waste of their time. I considered the feedback a reflection of their level of discomfort, stood by the approach, and wasn't too surprised when they later did a complete U-turn. And provided a glowing testimonial about how I saw through the noise of EDI initiatives and allowed the Board to have the information it needed to drive meaningful and lasting change. I was confident they'd get there, and grateful my client (the CPO) trusted me.

The lesson I took from that Board meeting was to deliver a Conscious Inclusion masterclass for leadership teams as early as possible, to provide everyone with a baseline understanding, before presenting the strategy.

Decision 6:
Give permission to yourself and others

If the inclusion conversation is stalling amongst the leadership team, fear not. It often surprises people when I say inclusion doesn't have to be led from the top.

There's a ton you can do to make your organisation more inclusive, even when everyone isn't on the same page yet.

Someone I learnt a huge amount from was Katrina in my team at Sky. She'd worked there for a few years before me, was incredibly well networked and her brain worked in all kinds of ways mine didn't. She expressed concern that we didn't have the final approval from the Exec, the night before launching the inclusion vision to 24,000 people across the company. She was right. Don't get me wrong, there'd been lots of rich discussion (and many PowerPoint presentations), we just didn't have that final green light. I paused... and realised there were no red lights either, so I asked if she thought we had done enough research? She said yes. Then I asked if we'd got enough feedback from every part of the business. She said yes. Next, I asked if she thought anyone else in Sky would be more confident about the plan than us? She said no. And my final question – did she think anything we were about to do would cause more harm than good? As she said no, a smile started spreading across her face. I matched that smile and said, then let's keep going until someone says stop.

> " *There's a ton you can do to make your organisation more inclusive, even when everyone isn't on the same page yet.*

And we realised the permission we'd granted ourselves was the exact permission we wanted everyone to grant themselves when they chose to get involved.

Decision 7:
Boost peer-to-peer learning

Learning about something unfamiliar from someone you know at work is a learning experience that tends to stick with you long after the event.

Everyone has something to teach you.

I still remember the day a colleague and friend got up on stage and shared her story of domestic abuse, post-traumatic stress, and healing, to raise awareness of the impact of mental health at work. It was emotional and led to many colleagues sharing their gratitude to her for shining a light on something they had also been through.

> " *Everyone has something to teach you.*

On another occasion, a Black colleague shared his pride in being best man at his friend's wedding. On the day, his friend's mother (White) asked him if his parents were slaves. It ruined the rest of what should have been a joyous occasion for him. He described it as a microaggression, which is a small and subtle act (often unintended) that signals you're 'other' or 'less than', which can have a significant cumulative impact when it happens repeatedly throughout your life. After the group he'd shared this experience with expressed their shock and empathy, they said it sounded more like blatant racism, as she'd assumed all Black people over a certain age must have been brought to the country as slaves.

Let's talk about race
The most impact I've ever seen for a workplace learning experience was for the *Let's talk about race* sessions designed and delivered by employees at Sky.

The idea came from three of us having lunch because we'd all recently read the book *Why I'm No Longer Talking to White People About Race* by Reni Eddo-Lodge and wanted to share our reflections. There was Harpreet: British, Punjabi and Brown; Lou: New Zealander, White with Black family; and me: British, White, and leading inclusion for the company.

The three of us talked openly about the learnings we'd taken from the book, how it had confronted us to reflect on our own experiences, and how comfortable (or not) the people around us were when talking about race. We realised we were learning even more from each other, and it sparked an idea from Lou to create a bigger conversation.

Harpreet approached a colleague in the learning and development team to create a 'Sky'ified' session. And I asked each of the HR Business Partners if they could find one or two people per department who wanted to facilitate. All they needed was a desire to be part of a change, with the willingness to hold a judgement-free space for participants. They didn't need any facilitation experience, as we provided a train the trainer session and matched people up with someone who had already run a session.

The demand was huge. Directors invited the facilitators to join them at their leadership meetings and I've never read such emotive feedback. Leaders described it as the most powerful session they'd ever been part of. The messages landed personally because people they knew had shared their wild variety in life experiences, purely because of the colour of their skin and cultural heritage.

The facilitators had each written down an experience that happens to them over and over again (microaggression), describing how it feels and the cumulative impact – a bit like one itchy insect bite, versus having bites all over your body. Part of the session was for leaders to read out loud one of the microaggressions and discuss. Examples included being asked if they eat curry on Christmas day, having their name repeatedly mis-pronounced, yet people have no problem learning names like Tchaikovsky and Beethoven, and constantly being mixed up with another person of the same ethnicity.

Being a media company, another part of the session was to talk movies and news headlines. Facilitators would often personalise the content, and conversation might have been about Black people continually being cast as the dangerous people in movies. And that leading to people locking their car doors or crossing the street when they see someone Black in their everyday life. Or how news headlines are often more favourable when someone White has done something wrong. The unintended subliminal message to individuals watching TV is White people are better.

The facilitators met regularly to discuss what worked, any reflections and what they could do to evolve the sessions. I took care of marketing and targeted departments that had significant gaps in experience between ethnicities reported in their engagement survey results (see Decision 26).

Those sessions quickly multiplied, extending to whole departments and every part of the business, and more and more facilitators got involved because they could see the impact. It was a huge ask, and a great career booster. Volunteers took part in landmark conversations, gained exposure to leaders across the business, and grew their network of Black and Brown people. I loved seeing those relationships develop, and how everyone cheered each other on when they were nervous or had decided to go for a promotion.

It's important to say here, that it's <u>not</u> the responsibility of people from underrepresented groups to teach those who are from overrepresented groups about prejudice, so you can't just expect this to happen. You will need to demonstrate a sincere commitment to building an inclusive organisation and support anyone brave enough to do it.

Decision 8:
Encourage respectful disagreement

How often have you been in a meeting where the most confident person gets their idea backed, and concerns expressed by others are quickly dismissed as being negative or not open-minded enough? Or, maybe, people don't speak up at all because they're fatigued by having their contribution routinely overlooked?

In my experience, the colleagues who haven't felt welcome or been encouraged to speak up have usually made astute observations and any concerns or alternative ideas they have are worth finding out about.

Psychological safety

Psychological safety is created when everyone in the team can contribute without a fear of being punished or ridiculed. Each member of the team feels respected and knows the value of hearing all ideas and concerns, so they can learn from each other and increase their ability to succeed.

Bias

Below are a few of the biases that might be fuelling your unconscious thinking. It's not a complete list; some might resonate more than others and you'll be influenced by different things at different times. Same goes for everyone you work with.

- **Affinity** – a preference to gravitate toward people who appear to be similar. This could influence your decisions in meetings, choosing suppliers etc.

- **Availability** – relying on recent or easily available information as a shortcut when evaluating something you're working on. People with different experiences and information may have a completely different evaluation.

- **Anchoring** – relying too heavily on the first piece of information. For example, being led by one person dismissing a problem, when others later tell you that that there is a problem.

- **Conserving** – maintaining a belief despite new evidence. This one can happen when engagement survey scores are lower than expected, for example suggesting that the survey was done at the wrong time of year. It's better to acknowledge the results are a snapshot of that moment in time and take action as needed.

- **In-group** – being more likely to support the people you are closest to and their ideas. It's a bit like playing favourites and could make anyone outside that inner circle feel like an outsider.

When you notice these biases showing up during discussions, you can encourage the team to adopt a set of similar questions to encourage respectful disagreement and extend each other's thinking. Here are some examples:

> " *When encouraging respectful disagreement, you're inviting people to assess the idea, not the person who presented it.*

- What does everyone else think?
- What would be the risk if we get this wrong?
- What other perceptions do people have?
- What alternative ideas could we consider?

- What else is on your minds?

When encouraging respectful disagreement, you're inviting people to assess the idea, not the person who presented it.

I like, I like, I wonder
I remember taking part in an idea's generation session. The group was divided into small teams and each team was given instructions to come up with their best idea before presenting it to the other groups for feedback.

Usually, I take care to deliver any critical feedback in a way that's encouraging to avoid knocking a person's self-esteem. But that day I was tired. My patience and curiosity were limited, and I had the potential to be sceptical about anything new or unfamiliar. The risk was that I'd deliver all my feedback in a negative way, which probably wouldn't have felt that great when the other groups presented their ideas.

Thankfully the facilitators provided a useful construct for giving feedback to each other. We were asked to identify two things we liked about each group's idea, and one thing we wanted to know more about to better understand how it could work. When we verbalised our feedback, our sentences started with:

- I like...
- I like...
- I wonder...

That method reframed my low-energy thinking and set me up to provide encouraging feedback, even if I disagreed.

Reflection section

Key decision themes

- Helping people better understand EDI happens one conversation at a time.

- There's plenty you can do without it being led from the top.

- It is <u>not</u> the responsibility of people from underrepresented groups to teach people from overrepresented groups.

- You can use familiar questions and feedback methods to make it safe to disagree and speak up without fear of being punished or ridiculed.

Questions to answer before we move on

- What are you afraid of when it comes to EDI?

■ What does being brave look like for you?

■ How can you boost psychological safety with your team?

Challenge automatic (biased) thinking

Remember the text I have as a screensaver? *Unless you're consciously including people, you're almost certainly unconsciously excluding people.* I still catch myself out, but I don't panic anymore as I know unconscious thinking is a huge part of how our brains work. With a fair bit of practice, I've learnt how to make my thinking conscious when needed and the next few decisions will help you to do it too.

Decision 9:
Slow down when making big decisions

Our brains are incredible machines, and it's estimated over 90% of our thinking is automatic. This is incredibly useful to navigate our busy lives and make quick decisions; yes or no, safe or dangerous, familiar or unfamiliar etc. The trouble is all brains are flawed with bias, so when it comes to making decisions about people, we need to use the 5–10% part of our brain that is slower, more thoughtful and goes and seeks research. Otherwise, just take the familiar or unfamiliar scenario, it could mean you create a commercial agreement with people you've spent more time with and overlook more lucrative propositions with people you've invested less time in building relationships with.

Daniel Kahneman is an Israeli-American psychologist and economist. He was awarded the 2002 Nobel Memorial Prize in Economic Sciences for his work on the psychology of judgement and decision-making, as well as

> **"** *Knowing how your mind operates will highlight when you might need to switch into system 2 and consider alternative perspectives.*

behavioural economics. And in his book *Thinking Fast and Slow*, he describes us having two systems:

- **System 1** runs the show most of the time, with automatic thinking and little effort, using the information that's right in front of you, and follows your first impressions and emotions to get to a speedy decision.
- **System 2** requires effort, is more thoughtful and goes and seeks research to explore the best option.

Knowing how your mind operates will highlight when you might need to switch into system 2 and consider alternative perspectives.

Extend thinking in group decisions
A tech team realised their Monday morning meetings, where all the big priority decisions for the week ahead were made, were attended entirely by men. To gain input from the other half of the population and prioritise the work, everyone invited a female

direct report to attend those meetings and extend the group's thinking. New voices in the group meant more perspectives contributing and that led to better decisions.

In my own work, I map out all the people I'd like to gather input from, then review the names to see if they're all a bit like me. And when they are, I spend a little more time thinking about which perspectives and life experiences I'm missing, and who I could approach to get a more complete picture to inform my work. I did it when gathering feedback about this book.

<u>Sleep on it</u>
I find Kahneman's work fascinating, and my dear friend Sam recently pointed out my preference to switch out of system 1 when I'm feeling the pressure. She noticed that whenever I'm faced with an emotional urge to react, I sleep on it, then wake up and look for new perspectives. I definitely haven't always been that way. A previous version of me was much more impulsive and suffered the consequences later. I live and learn.

Decision 10: Redefine what a good leader is

Next time you browse a book shop, have a look at how the authors are classified according to their gender. You'll often find books about being self-aware, collaborative and visionary that have been written by women are put in the self-help section. But such books written by men are found in the business section. And many of the *business* books written by men are filled with stories about other men and what can be learned from male sports teams. There's little or no mention of women.

Every book I've ever been given or recommended to read for business was written by a man. If you're a regular reader, see if you can spot any similar trends in your reading library. And watch out for the pesky algorithms next time you're making an online purchase, as they tend to recommend '*more books we think you'll like*' based on the selections you've made so far.

Leadership programmes
When you attend leadership programmes or transformation events, how many of the inspirational quotes that are put up on screen or printed in handouts feature women and people from underrepresented groups?

I'll guess, not many.

You usually hear from Henry Ford, Richard Branson, Albert Einstein, Jack Welch, Bill Gates, Stephen Covey... you get the picture. The White men are significantly overrepresented.

In case you're in any doubt about who else might inspire you, here's a few names off the top of my head: Maya Angelou, Brené Brown, Indra Nooyi, Edith Cowan,

Nelson Mandela, Nova Peris, Deborah Meaden, Whitney Wolfe Herd, Martin Luther King, Margaret Heffernan, Michelle Obama, Barack Obama, Jacinda Ardern, Malala Yousafzai, Greta Thunberg, Francesca Gino, Claire Balding, Mary Portas, Sara Blakely, Caroline Criado Perez, Sheryl Sandberg, Billie Jean King, Serena Williams. I could keep going.

Now consider how all those leadership development programmes have been built. Were they based on the leaders that came before? Is the research on what a good leader looks like based on a narrow section of leaders? When you turn up to the room or zoom, do the attendees share similar attributes?

If you answer yes to these questions, your leadership development investment is perpetuating a limited profile of leader. That's harming your commitment to inclusion and limiting the potential for your organisation.

The subliminal message for anyone who doesn't meet that narrow profile and is 'lucky enough to be there' (said with lots of sarcasm) is '*to get ahead here, it's ok if you look diverse, but you need to behave like the overrepresented group we've based all our research on*'. Leaders who do meet the narrow profile aren't seeing and feeling that inclusion is a priority for your business to remain relevant in the future.

And if you're talking about innovation, culture or how to be the best version of yourself without inclusion woven into the fabric of that content, you're not setting leaders up to respond to the fears and collective trauma of global events such as Me Too, Black Lives Matter or Eco-anxiety.

> " *How you define a leader affects who gets career development and promotions. And that can be a barrier to diversity.*

How you define a leader affects who gets career development and promotions. And that can be a barrier to diversity.

Decision 11:
Build inclusion reminders into routine discussions

Inclusion reminders are the way to nudge your brain into that 5–10% conscious thinking, to help you make more reliable and inclusive decisions. Without having to remember to do it.

Look through your annual calendar and make a note of any activity where you routinely make decisions about people. Remember this can be employees or customers. Here are some examples:

- Reviewing client accounts
- New business development
- Annual partnerships
- Deciding performance ratings
- Succession planning for critical roles
- Shortlisting the annual recognition awards

Next, get hold of the process documents and support materials and edit those notes to set clear guidance about when in the process you want people to consider diversity. The inclusion reminder should have 3–5 questions to reflect on before making a final decision.

Succession planning

We'll use succession planning as an example. A typical process guides you to identify people with the potential to take on more senior jobs or fill business-critical roles and decide what you'll do to develop their skills.

Inclusion reminder – once you've identified all the people, ask yourselves these questions:

1. How many women and people from underrepresented groups are on that list?
2. Does it feel right?
3. Who haven't you considered?
4. What can you do to include a more diverse mix?
    -   You might easily reevaluate the names you already have and/or sponsor more people in their career development

These inclusion reminders become key learning points in team discussion, and when captured in guidance notes, mean your brain doesn't need to worry about remembering how biased it is. Marvellous!

Decision 12:
Build a routine to find out what everyone really thinks

Which? is a company that tests products, offers independent consumer advice and highlights inferior products or services. And they have a fantastic meeting construct and evaluation technique to find out what everyone is _really_ thinking when discussing priorities for the business. I've shamelessly stolen it (all the best work is, why duplicate?), shared it with other clients, and I'm sharing it here with you too.

Voice in the room

Ahead of a Conscious Inclusion masterclass I ran with the leadership team, we defined the intent by answering what we wanted people to know, feel and do (like the message structure in Decision 2). We used that to write a question for participants to answer at the start of the session so we could bring everyone's voice into the room.

We wanted people to:

- **Know:** what the inclusion roadmap looked like for the next 12 months.
- **Feel:** energised, informed and confident about investing in the right areas.
- **Do:** take specific action on results of the company-wide inclusion diagnostic and engage people who hadn't already been involved.

And that led us to define:

- **The session intention** – 'Provide an opportunity to reflect on your impact as an inclusive leader.'
- **The voice in the room question** – 'When thinking about EDI, what is your biggest fear and proudest moment?'

Both the session intention and voice in the room question were shared in advance, so everyone knew what to expect and could consider their response. On the day, the session intention was reshared and we started with everyone sharing their fears and proudest moments. Within 15 minutes everyone was aware of each other's thoughts and the similarities and variations amongst those thoughts. That information was built on and referred to throughout the time spent together.

How Useful, Most Useful, More Useful (HU,MU,MU)
The masterclass concluded with HU,MU,MU questions to gather feedback. Within a few seconds people shared a score out of 10 for **how useful** the time had been when considering the session intention. Then we took a couple of minutes for people to describe the **most useful** part of the session to understand what had resonated most and anchor any personal learning. In the final few minutes, people described what would be even **more useful** next time we discussed this topic. This verified people's motivation and where they wanted to build confidence.

HU,MU,MU works so well, I often use it when facilitating discussions, so I can extend my learning and make the content I use more meaningful for each audience.

Reflection section

Key decision themes

- Over 90% of our decisions are automatic (unconscious).

- How you define a leader affects who gets career development and promotions and that can restrict diversity.

- You can prompt people with inclusion reminders in process notes to slow down their thinking and make more inclusive decisions (conscious).

- Defining the session intention and a 'voice in the room' question is a great way to hear from every voice at the start of a meeting. And HU,MU,MU helps you find out what people really thought at the end.

Questions to answer before we move on

- How many of your regular meetings have people with a similar demographic profile?

- When you consider the people who are being invested in to develop their skills, what's the mix of diversity?

- Which processes where you make decisions about people would you like to build in an inclusion reminder?

Supercharge employee networks

Employee networks are a community of volunteers formed by employees who've spotted an opportunity to support each other and make working at your organisation better. They can influence your approach to colleague, customer and community impact, so I think of them as having superpowers.

Decision 13:
Define what a network is (and isn't)

<u>A collective voice</u>
Their shared background and life experiences, combined with the understanding of your organisation purpose and goals, establishes them as a valuable collective voice, to guide you on the things that matter most.

And the most successful networks create more than a shopping list of issues for someone else to solve; they provide valuable insight into your biggest challenges and opportunities.

<u>A place to belong</u>
Often their primary purpose was to create a safe space for people to find more people just like them, when they've found themselves being the 'only' in their usual

meetings and teams. Joining a group like this can feel like finding that place where you belong.

A colleague once described the value of being part of a network in relation to their home life. Their family was struggling to accept their partner, due to them having a different cultural heritage. During that time, work and the network itself had been a real comfort to connect with colleagues who could relate.

> **"** *Networks don't tend to have the skill or autonomy required to make organisational changes, and they usually all have day jobs, so it would be a mistake to consider making delivery of the EDI plan their responsibility.*

Networks don't tend to have the skill or autonomy required to make organisational changes, and they usually all have day jobs, so it would be a mistake to consider making delivery of the EDI plan their responsibility.

Decision 14:
Educate as you celebrate notable dates

The first year of a network tends to focus on raising awareness that they exist so others can join, and hosting events to celebrate difference. Those events provide an opportunity to educate people about cultural heritage, history, traditions, and plenty more.

<u>Lead and seed</u>
There's a huge variety of national and international dates that can be marked to create an elevated moment of learning. It's worth agreeing at the start of each year which dates are most meaningful to the people who'd like to get involved in delivering events and key messages.

Each year, I recommend each network does a maximum of two big events. Think fewer, bigger, better. These are your 'lead' moments.

For all the other key dates and festivals, you can encourage people to mark them in their own way by utilising communication channels to share personal blogs, articles, research and videos. These are your 'seed' moments. Depending on your platform capability, this could turn into a pretty cool searchable learning library that gets better each time someone posts.

<u>Distributed teams</u>
In organisations where people work across a range of locations, anything that feels head office centric attracts the feedback of not feeling overly inclusive. So, you want to design your 'lead' events to welcome and involve everyone. Sharing event dates and any supporting materials in advance allows each site to self-serve and personalise the occasion. There's a watch out here, as telling them last minute tends to leave people feeling like they were forgotten.

For guest speakers, you can make it a virtual event so everyone joining has the same experience. Or you might live stream the speaker from one location, with local hosts organising a space to get together and watch on a big screen. Remember the snacks and record it, so people can tune in later if the event clashes with other commitments in their calendar.

It's important to say here that celebrating notable dates can't be the entirety of your EDI plan. Events can be a great way to learn, but they won't help you embed the sustainable change that's needed to make your organisation more inclusive.

Decision 15:
Sponsor network success

The value a senior sponsor can bring to a network is enormous. You can combine your knowledge and status to boost their level of impact.

Structure

The first step is to help them get their structure right. Networks can be made up of a mix of Chairs or Co-chairs, and lead roles for events, communications and external partnerships. Make sure there's a diverse mix in the leading roles, just as you should in any other leadership team. This means avoiding the women's network only being led by White women, the LGBT+ network by gay men, the religious network by Muslims etc.

Ambition

Next, help them shape their ambition. Here are three ways to do that:

1. Elevate their strategy – understand what they want to achieve for the members of the network. Then help them to create an outrageous ambition, simplify the actions, and prioritise them.

2. Coach network leads for success – help them combine career development goals with network ambition. Then challenge any thinking that doesn't work toward those goals.

3. Clear the path – navigating an organisation can be tricky to find the right person and know how to get things done. Ask what challenges they're facing, and how you can help.

Budget

Provide a budget to each network that aligns with the impact they plan to make and clarify how to access it. The amount may vary each year and differ by network depending on maturity and context. Budget will typically cover catering at events, guest speakers, benchmarking, and partnerships with external organisations.

Advocate for change

The most successful network sponsors not only boost the network's success, they advocate for organisation change when they're back in the rooms of power and influence.

Decision 16:
Get people involved in their own way

A familiar challenge for new networks is new members wanting to know how they can get involved. The founding members have put a ton of energy into the strategy and launch, and they've hosted an event encouraging people to join. But when people ask what they can do, the founders struggle to identify specific tasks.

A good way to overcome this is to map out a 12-month plan with specific objectives to deliver. Then pick two or three things that you could ask people to do that would help meet that objective and include it in all your communications. I call this 'channelling people's enthusiasm'.

Here is an example of three objectives for a new network, with three suggestions for how people could get involved.

Objective 1: Raise awareness of the network so people know they can join

- Add the network logo to your email signature
- Come along to events
- Join conversations on digital platforms

Objective 2: Let network members know what support is available

- Write a blog about your experience
- Design and maintain the network digital pages
- Write the network newsletter

Objective 3: Provide access to senior leaders to inspire people in their careers

- Organise an event for network members
- Nominate yourself as a speaker
- Nominate a colleague as a speaker

You'll notice there is a range in the level of investment involved. The menu not only provides a list of options, it also helps members understand the objectives of the network. This helps new members decide if and how they'd like to get involved and saves network leads responding to multiple similar queries.

The role of allies

The role of an ally is to support people from under-represented groups and use their privilege to raise awareness of the challenges they face. Allies can play a significant role in network success by showing up to events, recommending people join, and advocating for change in their usual work when relevant.

Networks can create specific guidance to help allies to champion underrepresented groups in their everyday interactions and respond to the challenges most often discussed between members. For example, a microaggression often faced by women is being interrupted or spoken over in meetings, so male allies could be encouraged to speak up when it happens and redirect the conversation by saying something like, '*before we move on, Rory, let's finish hearing what Nadine has to say*'. Or an LGBT+ ally can speak up when the advertising for a car seat is being scripted for a mother and father, by saying '*let's make sure this appeals to all families*'.

> " *When people have clear guidance about what's needed and how they could do it, it makes it much easier to get involved.*

When people have clear guidance about what's needed and how they could do it, it makes it much easier to get involved.

Decision 17:
Encourage collaboration for greater impact

Networks are ready-made collaboration and research groups, and if you're responsible for marketing, research, technology, or anything related to people, it's a good idea to build a relationship with network leaders. Then every time you're developing something new, you can combine your department skill with real lived experiences, to make sure you create something that works well for everyone.

Organisation impact

I owe a huge part of the successes we delivered at Sky to the collaboration with employee networks. During my time, the Parents' Network influenced parental leave and pay, the Armed Forces Network influenced the signing of the Military Covenant to become a Forces Friendly organisation, and the Body & Mind Network influenced almost every department to make a pledge toward raising awareness and reducing stigma for mental health. Networks also had an impact on what happened on screen with the *Rainbow Laces* campaign celebrating LGBT+ people in sport, and TV content collections to mark International Women's Day and Black History Month.

That's just a handful of examples and none of that success happened overnight. Some of those networks had been around for seven years and had developed a superstrength at mobilising for impact. The longer-standing networks were in a great position to inspire the newer networks. Leaders from each network met monthly to support each other with struggles, share their plans and make sure their key event dates didn't clash.

Network to network collaboration

Not only did they deliver side by side, they also collaborated to avoid things like International Women's Day or Mental Health Awareness Week looking and feeling like it was only focused on heterosexual White people. It happens.

And the big one was National Inclusion Week (NIW), which happens during the last week in September here in the UK. The platform was created by an organisation called Inclusive Employers in 2013 and each year they announce a theme for organisations to celebrate progress and inspire further action by learning from each other. NIW became an elevation moment in the annual calendar at Sky as it's about everyone. And we were delighted when Inclusive Employers approached us to be the first corporate sponsor in 2018. We were also nervous as we knew we were far from perfect. But with a little reassurance that sponsoring was much more about sharing than saying *'look at us, we've nailed it'*, we jumped at the opportunity.

That year the theme was *everyday inclusion*, and this was our message structure:

- **Headline message:** Sky is all in for inclusion
- We want people to:
    - **Know:** we're an industry leader.
    - **Feel:** like part of a community with people everywhere making a difference.
    - **Do:** make a pledge to do one thing that'll make a difference to the people you work with.

The message structure was shared repeatedly, far and wide (remember the heartbeat and lighthouse analogies in Decision 2). And people were encouraged to bring it to life in the way that resonated most to their teams and their work. People in every network, every department and every location worked towards it.

Colleagues were invited to share what they were doing in virtual meetings, so that people from every location could join (this was before Covid). NIW was no place for hierarchy or being head office centric, and the meetings provided an opportunity for feedback and inspiration. Some ideas were taken even further, and others were naturally filtered out, when we could see something better was emerging.

The spirit of collaboration for hundreds of people who had mostly never met each other was inspiring. Providing a simple message structure, and the freedom to get creative, generated more action than anyone could ever have imagined.

> " *Providing a simple message structure, and the freedom to get creative, generated more action than anyone could ever have imagined.*

We had video messaging, TV guests, thousands of pledges being made in staff restaurants, music playlists on Spotify, selfies on social media, blogs, inclusion lanyards (branded lanyards were like currency at Sky), inclusion pledges, inspirational speakers at events and so much more.

So, when you're aiming to do something big, bring multiple minds together, create the path, provide guidance, then get out of the way. And when everyone involved pulls it off, be sure to celebrate their success.

For the control freaks out there, I see you. I am you. Try letting go.

Decision 18:
Be specific about the 'give and get' exchange

Now you've read just some of the value sponsored networks can bring to your organisation, it's right to consider the investment you'll give in return.

My recommendation is to give time rather than money, because when you pay networks, there's a risk that the organisation will cut that headcount when budgets are reviewed. Or, worse, dictate what will be delivered. Giving time protects the integrity of a network and their ability to provide a collective voice about the things that aren't working and need to change.

Let's say you give network chairs and people doing lead roles one day a month during operational hours. Those 12 days can be used to motivate a network of champions, deliver an event, make a submission to an external benchmark, or review the objectives for the following year. Some might draw down their 12-day allocation in hours throughout the year, and others might use them more intensively.

A yearly allocation provides a framework for line managers to support each person's ambition and be confident their day job will still get done. And for network chairs it's a helpful expectation to set when someone expresses interest in taking on a lead role. It's useful to think of the allocation less about monitoring and more about guidance.

For a network with two co-chairs and two leads, that amounts to 4 people x 12 days = 48 days a year. Imagine what's possible with 48 days dedicated to purpose and action.

Reflection section

Key decision themes

- Employee networks can supercharge success in your organisation, but it would be a mistake to consider making delivery of the EDI plan their responsibility.

- Celebrating notable dates is great for learning but shouldn't be the entirety of your EDI plan.

- Senior sponsors can bring enormous value, and advocate for change back in the rooms of power and influence.

- Make it easy for people to get involved.

- Providing a simple message structure and the freedom to get creative can generate a huge impact.

- Give time rather than money to protect network integrity.

Questions to answer before we move on

- How easy is it for new hires to find a network and join?

- Which departments could benefit from collaborating with networks?

- What recognition do networks get?

Share the spotlight and unite people

Events and communications set the tone for how people think and feel about your organisation. And you can influence that in everything from annual conferences and weekly meetings to daily messages and interactions.

Decision 19:
Create a stage for the modern age

If you consider the last three industry events, town halls or global leadership meetings, who were the people that made the announcements and shared updates? Who was the compere? Who were the experts?

<u>Recommend and sponsor</u>
Unless you're deliberate about it in planning, the line-up of speakers is often a bit similar, and once you see it, you can't unsee it. If that's the case, next time you're planning to host an event write down everyone you can think of that would be excellent to put on stage and see if you have a diverse mix. If not, ask those people you first wrote down to recommend and sponsor

> " Unless you're deliberate about it in planning, the line-up of speakers is often a bit similar, and once you see it, you can't unsee it.

someone with a different demographic that would also be excellent, and perhaps hasn't had their first shot yet.

This happened to me back in 2017. A colleague two layers up in the hierarchy was approached to speak at a summit event in California and they couldn't go, so they suggested me as I had great insight to share from a mix of industries. They gave me guidance and feedback on my content, and another colleague made my slides look snazzy. I was so nervous and, at the same time, thrilled they believed in me. I represented women less polished and less senior. The audience were warm and responsive, and I realise now, that was the start of my speaking career!

Pass the mic

Today I'm regularly invited to speak at events, and always ask who the other speakers are. If they all look a bit like me, I decline and recommend someone else that could make their event better reflect the audience. When we get to the tech rehearsal for a mixed panel, if I notice all the White people speak first, I suggest a different running order. This is known as '*passing the mic*' and I'd encourage you to do the same when you spot the opportunities.

Balance the biographies

Another watch out is the way speakers are described in promotion materials. I shared an observation with an event host who'd invited three of us to speak at a leadership launch event. The materials described me as an '*Advisor*', the other women as a '*Specialist*', and the man as '*Founder of his own business*'. We were all founders of our own businesses. They were grateful for the feedback, made the change and committed to reviewing all future materials for similar bias.

Decision 20:
Ask what people need when attending events

Getting lots of people together for celebrations, launching new products and sharing plans can be wonderful for boosting an inclusive culture.

You need to ask people what they need when you're making plans, so you can be sure to make everyone welcome.

These are some of the things your guests might be worried about:

- Personal safety and getting home late at night.
- Being able to get into the venue and toilets with mobility aids.
- Knowing the buffet won't be risky (unlabelled food) or lacking if you have allergies or dietary requirements.
- Wondering if it's a booze fest and your only option is fizzy drinks. If you're recovering from addiction, practising faith or pregnant, you may not want to attend events that encourage drinking.

- Having enough notice to plan around family commitments.

- The environment being overwhelming for people who are neurodiverse, nervous or introverted.

- Being hard of hearing or speaking multiple languages and needing subtitles when there are lots of speakers.

- Forced fun that's not aimed at you. For example, golf days in male-dominated teams, or one-size-fits-all costumes for different body shapes.

- Not being able to afford to split the bill when you have limited disposable income.

Asking people if they have any specific requirements can be as simple as including a free text box on your event registration form.

Team socials

I've known teams that rotate responsibility for organising team socials, so everyone gets a go and events are more varied. They were also full of gratitude when it wasn't their turn, especially the Executive Assistants, who could participate and enjoy without worrying about every detail.

Decision 21: Use language that unites people

Much like the world around us, the language we use is continually evolving, because what was deemed socially acceptable in the past may be harmful today.

Language has the power to bring us together... or perpetuate unhelpful stereotypes and divide people.

White news correspondents and journalists sparked outrage when covering Russia's war on Ukraine in 2022, for having described Ukraine as *'civilised'* (compared to other countries) and saying things like *'it's very emotional for me because I see European people with blue eyes and blond hair...being killed every day'*.

> **❝** *Language has the power to bring us together... or perpetuate unhelpful stereotypes and divide people.*

American writer, journalist and professor Moustafa Bayoumi said this in an opinion piece: *'These comments point to a pernicious racism that permeates today's war coverage... The implication is clear: war is a natural state for people of color, while White people naturally gravitate toward peace'*.[1]

In an open letter on the reporting of Ukraine, Marcus Ryder MBE wrote:

> *'Deaths in times of war are tragic wherever they occur, and we must avoid linking their importance, or how much sympathy we have for them, to their ethnicity or where they are based in the world'*.

'The current war in Ukraine could be a seminal moment in how newsrooms respect diversity and incorporate anti-racism into their work'.

'I implore all journalists to continue your excellent work while remembering our core values'.[2]

Everyday language

The language you use to communicate in meetings and informal conversations also has the power to unite people. And you want to avoid any narrative that suggests primary and secondary groups.

Here are some examples:

Instead of	Try	Benefit
Welcome ladies and gentlemen	Welcome everyone	More modern and gender neutral
Hey guys, it's good to see you	Hey everyone, it's good to see you	Gender neutral. I didn't see this one until someone asked me, 'When was the last time a heterosexual guy talked about dating a guy?'
When English isn't their first language...	When English is an additional language	Acknowledges additional brain processing and skill
Chairman	Chair or Chairperson	Gender neutral
Manmade	Humanmade	Gender neutral and can be used for present and past to acknowledge women having been so often erased from history[3]

He or she/his or her	They/their	Trans and non-binary friendly, gender neutral and no risk of misgendering someone Imagine you didn't see who left their umbrella in a café and when you hand it in, you say 'someone has left their umbrella'
Some people struggle with their mental health	When we struggle with our mental health	Instead of talking about 'those' people, acknowledge we all have mental health and help reduce stigma

Think 'we' and 'our' over 'us' and 'them'.

Decision 22:
Make your communications accessible

As well as providing translations for multiple languages, there are a whole bunch of tips to boost your internal and external communications, so more people can understand and enjoy them.

Writing style

- **Use white space, short sentences and para-graphs** to break up the sea of text, so readers can more easily absorb your content.

- Use **easy to read fonts** and keep them **left aligned** to be dyslexia friendly.

- Choose **simple language and avoid localised sayings or acronyms** to benefit people with dual languages, literal thinking styles and, frankly, people who can't be bothered to get out a dictionary. Your communication shouldn't be a comprehension test.

- When you're happy with it – **halve it and halve it again**. This one helps people with a short attention span. Just me?

Make it easy

My heart sinks a little when I receive any correspondence from the financial services (FS) industry. Understandably, FS is heavily regulated, but I recently received eight documents totalling 86 pages, to renew one policy. That level of information makes my brain shut down and leads to major procrastination. Thankfully I use an insurance broker and they're patient talking through the details, but it doesn't feel like a world designed with consumers in mind.

This year I also encouraged my mortgage lender to ask someone unfamiliar with the technical and traditional language of FS to review the voting materials they sent out to customers ahead of their Annual General Meeting. Because I'd had to look up several of the words before being able to respond confidently.

On a brighter note, Monzo Bank have published *Our tone of voice* and they describe it in a nutshell – *'We use the language our audience uses and make technical stuff as clear as we can'*.[4]

Let's all be more Monzo.

<u>Media</u>

- **Include subtitles on all your videos** for people with hearing impairments, working in open plan offices, and who travel for work.

- **Include different body shapes, height and ages** for characters as well as the usual mix of demographics.

- For the millions of people using screen reading technology to assist a visual impairment (more common as we get older):

  - Avoid text being embedded on top of images, so a screen reader can read it too.

  - #CapitaliseHashtags so the screen reader knows the start of each new word.

  - Include picture descriptions and make use of the 'Add Alt text' feature on social media and webpages.

All of these tips are simple to do and make your communication better for everyone. Why not create an inclusive communications standard and involve colleagues by asking what else you can include.

Decision 23:
Share talking and listening time in meetings

How often have you been in a meeting and one or two people dominate the conversation? Unless meetings are facilitated to hear a mix of perspectives, a lot of people think they're a waste of time because around

30% of people dominate 80% of the conversation. Assuming the right people are in the meeting, this imbalance could be due to perceived status, cultural differences in communication, personality types etc.

The power of introverts

American writer and author Susan Cain argues that modern Western culture misunderstands and under-values the traits and capabilities of introverted people, who are often reflective, great at listening and take time to make decisions. In her book *Quiet: The Power of Introverts in a World that Can't Stop Talking*, she says, '*For far too long, those who are naturally quiet, serious or sensitive have been overlooked. The loudest have taken over – even if they have nothing to say*'.

Facilitation guidance

When you're the person facilitating or chairing a meeting, here is some guidance to help more voices be heard and get more value from group conversations:

- Send an agenda in advance so everyone knows what's going to be discussed and has opportunity to consider their input. This could be three bullet points in the meeting invitation.

- Approach people directly ahead of the meeting and tell them the specific input you'd like them to share and explain why. This provides time to reflect and can also support newer people, or people with less confidence etc.

- In the moment, if Catherine is taking up too much airtime, say something like, 'great to get your input, Catherine... I'm keen to hear what other people are thinking'.

If you're the person bursting with ideas and feedback:

- Write them down until the conversation naturally comes to you, or for virtual meetings use the hands-up emoji.
- Notice your ratio of speaking/listening alongside the rest of the group and adjust if needed.

And if you notice people still aren't speaking up, ask them privately what you can do to create an environment where they're comfortable to participate.

Reflection section

Key decision themes

- Unless you're deliberate about it in planning, the line-up of speakers at an event is often a bit similar.

- There are a range of things your guests might be worried about when you invite them to an event.

- The language you choose has the power to bring people together (or divide people).

- Having an inclusion standard for all your communications means more people can understand and enjoy it.

- 30% of people can dominate 80% of meetings unless you manage it.

Questions to answer before we move on

- How diverse was the line-up of speakers at the last event you hosted or attended?

- How many of the tips in the **writing style** and **media** sections does your organisation already do?

- During the last meeting you attended what percentages of time did you speak and listen?

Part 4

How to embed inclusion into policies and process

HR holds many of the People Experience levers and in Part 4 we'll walk through how to weave inclusion into reporting, policies, flexible working, pay and benefits.

Use data to unlock sustainable progress

Insight drawn from data is a powerful motivator for change. It helps you understand what's happening and provides clear evidence about what's working and what's not. This helps you focus your energy in the right places. Combine quantitative data (numbers) with qualitative data (verbal or written) and you'll have everything you need to know whether your organisation is inclusive.

> *You can measure the impact of everything you're doing, and I'd go so far as to say, if you aren't measuring it, don't do it.*

You can measure the impact of everything you're doing, and I'd go so far as to say, if you aren't measuring it, don't do it.

Decision 24:
Work with subject matter experts

Getting an outside view on what you're doing can boost confidence and help you reset your priorities each year. I learnt so much from external organisations, who provided subject matter expertise, when we were establishing the right approach for inclusion at Sky.

A tiered approach

When choosing external sources for benchmarking your progress, I recommend the ones that have a tiered approach as they provide you with a clear path for progression. One example is the UK government's *Disability Confident* employer scheme, which is rigorous and easily accessible, particularly for smaller businesses.[1] It has three levels you can progress through:

- **Level 1 – Disability committed** – Agree to the Disability Confident commitments and identify at least one action you'll carry out to make a difference for disabled people

- **Level 2 – Disability confident** – Self-assess your organisation for hiring, developing and keeping people in your business

- **Level 3 – Disability leader** – Act as a disability champion in local and business communities

Competitive lists

At Sky, we took part in several EDI benchmarks that publish a list of the top organisations that year. They were great for generating a huge sense of pride for all the people involved in the work, particularly the *Inclusive Top 50*, which recognises inclusion for everyone.[2] And inviting people to the awards evenings was a wonderful way to thank people for their contribution.

The detailed feedback and case studies generated by these organisations were invaluable in prioritising actions for the year ahead and providing confidence we were heading in the right direction. The social media coverage and being able to display the benchmark badges on the careers page also helped demonstrate our commitment to inclusion.

When we hit the top spots in various lists, we understood those badges didn't mean we were perfect, and instead were recognition that our progress was a little further ahead than the other competitors that year. We also decided not to take part the following years because it didn't feel particularly inclusive to get to the top and stay there, preventing other organisations from getting their moment of glory.

Decision 25:
Collect good data and protect it

There are some universal challenges with diversity data, including incompleteness, trust, and what information can be collected in different parts of the world. You'll need to make sure you use data in accordance with local data protection legislation and protect people's private information. Here in the UK, we comply with the European General Data Protection Regulation (GDPR). When it landed in 2018 many organisations stopped collecting diversity data (uh-oh!) because they weren't using it to assess for fairness in their processes. The good news is you can legally collect most data for the purpose of monitoring equality, so long as you tell people how you use it and have appropriate governance in place.

Good data collection principles include:

<u>What to ask</u>

- Mirror the categories that are most widely used in your country/ies. In the UK it would be the UK Census, which captures population data every 10 years to plan for public services.

- Provide a *'prefer not to say'* option for each question. People choosing this tells you how much they trust what you're doing with the data, and it's better to have this information than have questions unanswered.

<u>How and when to ask</u>

- When you ask people to provide personal demographic information, explain how you will use that data and how that benefits them, as well as the organisation.

- Make it as easy as possible to complete. When people are applying for or starting a new job is the ideal time.

- Run an annual refresh campaign, to remind people to update their data following any life changes e.g., disabilities or becoming a parent. This is also good for reminding people who haven't already provided their information.

Processing the information

- Only ever report in aggregated groups of predetermined sizes e.g., a minimum of six. This means people's individual responses are always reported with others and will remain anonymous.

- Produce standardised reports to create one source of the truth. It's the safest option and avoids data protection rules being breached.

- Heavily restrict who has access to individual or 'raw' data and review that list at least annually.

Decision 26:
Report on inclusion

To see if you have an inclusive culture, you need to find out if people from underrepresented groups are having the same good experience as people from overrepresented groups. In surveys of any kind, the scores for underrepresented groups are often swallowed by the overrepresented if you only look at total scores. You need to understand how the scores differ for people from different demographic groups.

> 66 *To see if you have an inclusive culture, you need to find out if people from underrepresented groups are having the same good experience as people from overrepresented groups.*

Take an engagement survey, which is used to determine how happy, engaged or satisfied people are working for you. You might be pleased to see an overall score of 83% and feel confident no action is needed. To understand inclusion, you need to break that 83% down by characteristic e.g., ethnicity. You will likely find your largest population, let's say White people, are having a better time and their responses have generated a rating of 84%. And the ratings generated from your smaller populations of Black, South Asian, Mixed-race people etc. are only 59%, 62% and 65%. Their scores are being hidden because of the relative weighting of the largest population. And these scores paint a very different picture of how inclusive the organisation is.

Now let's say you overlay gender on top of race. You are likely to find the responses from Black men are generating a rating much lower than the responses from White men. This overlapping of two (or more) connected characteristics is known as intersectionality (see Part 1).

Even when your data is not complete, you can report results for the *'knowns'* alongside the *'unknowns'* to get the full picture of people's experience. So, at the highest level for disability you would report scores for people who:

1. are living with a disability (known)
2. have no disability (known)
3. haven't answered the question (unknown)
4. have responded *'prefer not to say'* (unknown)

If you have a high percentage of *'prefer not to say'* responses and those people are also reporting lower scores in your engagement survey, you'll need to focus on building trust before you can do anything else.

The level of insight you can obtain will depend on the systems and data insight capability your organisation has invested in. Your reporting is likely to start off basic, which helps to avoid overwhelming everyone. Start with version one and get more sophisticated as capability and confidence grow.

Ask more powerful questions

Since 2020 there has been a surge in engagement survey providers adding diversity and inclusion questions to meet demands from clients. Trouble is, I've yet to see anything that's adding real power because the questions seek a rating of '*perception*' rather than personal experience.

Instead of adding questions like '*This organisation is committed to diversity and inclusion*', or '*People here are treated fairly regardless of religion, disability*' etc., use questions that actually describe inclusion: being valued, heard and involved. They should start with 'I' to centre the individual, for example:

- 'I have good opportunities to learn'
- 'If I'm treated unfairly, I'd be comfortable speaking up'
- 'I have enough say in how to do my job'

Then, when you get the results, make sure to break them down by demographic. This is how to determine the differences in people's experiences.

You should break scores down in this way for each department if they're big enough to protect anonymity.

Seeing the scores for your area of responsibility, especially if there are large gaps in ratings between demographics, generates personal responsibility. I've seen gaps of over 20 points inspire leaders to create a much fairer and welcoming environment for their teams. And when those gaps shrank, not only were they proud, but they were also able to share their learning with other departments.

If you find overwhelming gaps, determine what <u>one</u> thing would make the biggest difference and focus on small improvements one at a time. A concept often described as making incremental gains. When you see progress and feel confident that momentum will continue, start the next thing.

Depending on the sensitive nature of the gaps, you might need to bring in someone neutral to facilitate a listening session and deliver you an unpolished summary of what's driving those very different ratings.

> *Putting all your effort on diversity without creating an inclusive environment creates a horrible experience for the underrepresented. It can make people feel like they're wanted because they're different but are expected to be the same as everyone else.*

If you haven't yet introduced any EDI reporting, understanding who does and doesn't feel valued, heard and involved is the place to start. Because putting all your effort on diversity without creating an inclusive environment creates a horrible experience for the underrepresented. It can make people feel like they're wanted because they're different but are expected to be the same as everyone else.

Decision 27:
Report on diversity at every level

When I ask clients how they would know when their organisation was fully inclusive, they tell me that they'd see a diverse mix of people at every level. I agree, so long as each demographic group is also having an equally good experience.

Start by dividing your organisation into layers of hierarchy and report the percentages of each demographic for each layer. Then compare those percentages to the census. This will highlight any areas of over and underrepresentation. If you have large enough departments, replicate the format for each team.

Decision 28:
Report on the recruitment process

Recruiters often get a hard time for not bringing in enough diverse candidates but data often shows it's the decisions made by hiring managers that's limiting progress. To see what's happening, report on candidate demographic at the application, shortlist and interview stages.

To supercharge the report, you can then show, based on current rates of recruitment and retention (e.g., over the last 12 months), when your organisation will reflect the community you serve. Some awesome colleagues at Sky blew my mind when I saw the information presented in this way. Again, break the data down if you have big enough departments to help hiring managers feel accountable.

Decision 29:
Report on people process outcomes

The most powerful step in exploring day-to-day bias is to report on how the outcomes of all your usual people processes vary for different demographic groups. At least once a year you should look at:

- performance ratings
- pay increases
- recognition awards
- promotions
- secondments

Don't forget retention
There's no point doing lots of work to bring people from underrepresented groups into the organisation if they're leaving at a disproportionate rate. So, make sure you also report on the outcomes by demographic for:

- resignations
- dismissal
- redundancies
- settlement agreements

This data can be confronting and provides valuable information to help shape the *inclusion reminders* (Decision 11) you can provide to people when conducting these activities.

> *Breaking data down by demographic group is the key to increasing awareness and unlocking sustainable progress.*

Breaking data down by demographic group is the key to increasing awareness and unlocking sustainable progress.

Do I sound like a broken record yet? I hope so.

Reflection section

Key decision themes

- Working with subject matter experts will help you determine your priorities each year.

- You can legally collect most demographic data for the purposes of monitoring equality, so long as you tell people how you use it and have the appropriate governance in place.

- Use questions that measure individual experience rather than perception in your engagement survey.

- Reporting on the diversity of applications, shortlists and interview will highlight if it's recruiters and/or managers that need support.

- Reporting on diversity at each level will highlight any areas of overrepresentation.

- Reporting on process outcomes will highlight any day-to-day bias.

Questions to answer before we move on

- What data is available in your organisation?

- How confident are you that useful insight is being drawn from it?

- What external investments do you have, or could you have to help guide your approach?

Evolve people policies to be human centred

The way your policies are written plays a big part in setting the tone for how much your organisation cares about people and the different experiences they have in life. If you've tended to introduce and update policies purely to keep up with what's required by law, this chapter will highlight plenty of things you can do to better reflect your commitment to inclusion.

Decision 30:
Go beyond employment law

Many of the policies I review don't reflect the actual human kindness many organisations offer when someone needs support. Take someone who is grieving a lost family member or someone who has a cancer diagnosis and needs intensive chemotherapy. Empathy kicks in and the line manager tells that person to take the time they need and not to give work a second thought until they're feeling better. Because they understand it will be one less thing to worry about.

But... the absence policy reads something like, *if you take too much time off, we'll discipline you and potentially terminate your employment.*

Imagine something tough happening in your life. You look up the policy, so you know what to expect, and instead of compassionate guidance, you're met with a message that pretty much says, *we don't care about you, because whatever is happening in your life is an inconvenience and stands in the way of the effective running of this organisation.*

Many policies are grounded in employment law, focus on what the organisation '*must*' do and how people will be '*handled*' if they break the rules. A lot like handling humans as resources to be managed.

I encourage you to review your policies and consider the many experiences your employees will have in life. Think about them as providing guidance and support for human 'beings' rather than rules to follow for human 'resources'. And for the occasional rogue employee, find out what's behind their behaviour, then support them and/or manage the disruption accordingly.

Decision 31:
Provide support for women, trans and non-binary people

More and more employers are now introducing support for women, trans and non-binary people who were socialised as women. They recognised their previous offering didn't provide very well for half the world's population. Historically, workplace policies have been '*one-size-fits-man*'.

Examples of new support and guidance cover period pain, endometriosis, gender transition, peri menopause and menopause.

Next time you think about your colleagues showing up every day, experiencing the wild things happening to their body, putting on a brave face and getting the job done, perhaps you'll marvel at how truly remarkable they are.

Decision 32: Mirror parental leaves

Families are created in many different ways including birth, surrogacy and adoption, with parents who are LGBT+, heterosexual or cisgender. There are usually multiple policies for employees to navigate to find out how much time they can take off and what pay is available. By mirroring all the different types of leave, you can make your parenthood policies more inclusive and much more user friendly.

Parental leave is out of date
Society still fundamentally expects women to prioritise childcare and men to prioritise work. It's not just policies in the workplace, it's also the location of public nappy changing facilities, community support, classes to prepare for parenthood, and the marketing for playgroups. It may not surprise you by now that I gave some inclusion feedback to my local council, who'd advertised 'mother' and baby sessions in the local magazine instead of 'parent' and baby, which would have been so much better.

Then there's our legal entitlements. Here in the UK, following the arrival of a child or children, mothers or primary* carers can take up to 52 weeks off with 90% of average weekly earnings for the first six weeks, then £156.66 statutory weekly pay (as at August 2022) for the next 33 weeks. The rest is unpaid. And fathers or secondary* carers can only take up to two weeks off with £156.66 statutory weekly pay.

Let that sink in. The difference in time allowed away from work is 50 weeks!!!

This positions women as first responders for all things family and puts pressure on men to be the breadwinner and earn more, more, more. It starts the minute you announce you're expecting. When a woman shares the news, she's asked '*How long are you taking off? Will you go part time? Have you found childcare yet?*' And when a man shares the news, the response is '*Congratulations that's awesome news, now let's discuss the transformation programme*'.

*primary and secondary is the gender-neutral language many organisations use to better include LGBT+ parents. I appreciate the intent but am actually not a fan because it suggests one parent is more significant than the other. Keep reading for how you could overcome this.

Dads want more time with their families

Many employers enhance their parental leave policies beyond the legal entitlements, yet still, most are weighted in favour of a '*primary*' parent. Of course, anyone who gives birth needs time to recover both physically and psychologically. Yet, for dual parent families, dads and secondary carers say two weeks is not enough.

Research conducted by *Working Mums* and *Pregnant Then Screwed* found:

- 80% of dads say their employer is not doing enough to support fathers.
- 46% have or would consider switching roles to access better parental leave and pay.
- 80% are only offered two weeks' paternity leave by their employer.
- 28% do not take the full two weeks.
- And 10% take no paternity leave at all, with more than half of those claiming it's because they couldn't afford to take it.[3]

In what world do we want to prevent fathers from bonding with their kids? Who does that benefit? It isn't the children.

> " *In what world do we want to prevent fathers from bonding with their kids? Who does that benefit? It isn't the children.*

When I collaborated with the Parents' Network at Sky as part of our research into how we might enhance our paternity leave, every dad and secondary carer told me the same thing: two weeks isn't enough. Their reasons included: their partner's body having just gone through something traumatic and needing more time at home to support them to recover, the overwhelm of learning to look after a baby or support siblings as family life shifted, their partners not being able to drive if they've had surgery, not being around to give emotional support as hormones were settling down, and almost unanimously a lack of sleep.

Life as they knew it had forever changed and they all felt huge guilt at going back to work so soon. They wanted access to flexible working, particularly when the birth was approaching and when they initially returned to work.

That first upgrade to the paternity policy was a few years ago now, and we moved it from two weeks' paid leave, to six weeks' paid and six weeks' unpaid that could be taken any time in the first year. The response was overwhelming, and most people took the six weeks' paid leave and combined it with their annual leave, which was at least five weeks.

Many companies have gone further and offer six months' paid parental leave for *every* parent. They've blended all policies into one Parental Leave Policy, solving the language issue of '*primary*' and '*secondary*'. And they've done away with '*shared parental leave*', which in the UK had all the right intentions but the take-up is estimated to be between 2 and 8% because the marketing of the policy is poor, it's challenging to understand, and it requires the '*primary*' parent to sacrifice some of their recovery and adjustment time.[4]

Spotify

Spotify is just one of the companies who offer six months' leave with 100% pay, plus a seventh month for transitioning back to work.[5] Leave is available for any length of service, and it's for every parent in every country, which removes the barriers of different local legislation. Within six months, 186 employees had used the benefit, and out of the 29 employees in the US, 90% were male. That's hugely significant when you consider most states only offer 12 weeks' unpaid leave, which is unaffordable for most families and goes unused. Spotify's policies, and others like them, are helping to shift long-outdated cultural norms.

Smaller organisations with less money to spend

Not all businesses can afford the generosity of companies like Spotify, but they might still be able to take a significant step by mirroring the minimum legal entitlement traditionally offered to women. So, if we use the UK as an example, *any* parent could take up to 52 weeks off with 90% of average weekly earnings for the first six weeks, then £156.66 weekly pay for the next 33 weeks. And the rest unpaid.

The benefit to women

The benefits of mirroring parental leave go beyond providing the option for men to be an active parent. It creates a modern norm for planning for absence, flexing

> "To create the possibility of gender equity at work, you must create the possibility for it at home.

hours around commitments outside work, and shifting away from any expectation of always being available. This reduces the impact on women getting squeezed out of the workforce because of last-minute early and late meetings, work-related travel being required at short notice, or being passed over for promotion because it's perceived their career is less important to them now.

To create the possibility of gender equity at work, you must create the possibility for it at home.

Decision 33:
Introduce carers leave

Carers UK is a charity supporting carers with expert advice and support. They estimate that, across the UK, 6.5 million people are unpaid carers, supporting a loved one who is older, disabled or seriously ill.[6] That's one in eight adults. Whether it's a few hours a week or round the clock care, it can have a huge effect on people's lives. Every day 6,000 people become carers, and for some it's sudden due to illness or accident, while for others it creeps up as parents manage less well on their own or your partner's health gets gradually worse.

Insurance company Aviva provide 10 days' paid carers leave to help employees remain at work while caring.[7] Five days are allocated for planned leave and five for emergencies, which can be taken in as little as one-hour chunks. They also offer an additional eight weeks of unpaid carers leave, to reduce the likelihood of people having to lose their career and financial security when caring demands escalate. Since introducing the policy Aviva found one in seven employees has at least one form of caring responsibility, and on average they take 10 hours' paid leave across a year.

Introducing carers leave makes a massive difference to people doing some of society's most important and unrecognised work. And it'll help you keep brilliant people working for you, because they know you'll support them when times get tough.

Decision 34:
Remove length of service restrictions

A traditional approach that needs unpicking is providing better support for people who have been working for you for longer. We inherited this from a time when people used to stay with one employer for a long time, and prospective candidates would make their initial assessments about how good an employer was, then stay there.

If your enhanced maternity and paternity leave policies kick in after six months' service, the person that's worked for you for 4.5 months gets significantly less than the person who's worked for you for 6.5 months. Both are having a huge change in their life and will be needing time to adapt and bond.

The other disadvantage of organisations tying something as significant as parental leave to length of service is shackling people to your organisation, who stopped giving their best years ago. It also discourages people who are brilliant from applying to work for you if they're planning to grow their family. Because it's a financially risky jump having to first understand any potential new employer's policy and get the due date for delivery or adoption just right.

❝ Update any policies related to length of service and make them available to everyone from day one, to provide the same support for people sitting next to each other.

Update any policies related to length of service and make them available to everyone from day one, to provide the same support for people sitting next to each other.

Decision 35:
Use gender-neutral language

The shift here is to move away from language that assumes all people identify with the sex they were assigned at birth, and language that promotes heterosexuality as the '*normal*' orientation. So '*she*' or '*he*' becomes '*they*', '*her*' or '*his*' becomes '*their*' and '*mother*' or '*father*' becomes '*parent*'. You may find other updates that need to be made, such as '*chairman*', and you can refer to Decision 21 and work with your networks to find the right approach.

I joined Dr Naveen Puri on a panel for a Bupa Health Insights event and loved how he spoke about cancer screening. He described doctors taking an organ-specific approach e.g., cervixes and prostates, to navigate which tests are appropriate for the individual.[8] This was a deliberate decision to include trans and non-binary people, as the data shows the take-up for cancer screening was much lower in these populations when compared with cisgender patients. Not surprising when the medical profession traditionally talked about 'women's' health and 'men's' health.

Using gender-neutral language in your policies normalises language that includes everyone.

Decision 36:
Demonstrate zero tolerance to harassment and bullying

Responding quickly and appropriately when someone reports bullying or harassment is a fundamental ingredient for inclusion.

Your policy needs to demonstrate commitment to providing an environment where people are treated, and treat others, with dignity and respect. It should apply to employees and everyone else you hold relationships with e.g., contractors, clients, service users, customers etc.

It's useful to provide examples of what won't be tolerated at your organisation as people's personal awareness and experiences in other organisations will vary. Here are some examples:

- Unwanted physical contact such as hugging
- Unwelcome sexual advances or suggestive language or behaviour
- Sending offensive emails, text messages or social media content
- Mocking or belittling a person's demographic characteristic e.g., disability, ethnicity, faith, age or sexual orientation
- Purposely and repeatedly misgendering some-one
- Purposely excluding a colleague from social events deliberately or thoughtlessly, for example, due to them being a parent, homosexual or Muslim
- Physical or psychological threats

Alternative routes of reporting

If informal requests to stop the bullying or harassment aren't working or there is a lack of support from the immediate line manager, provide an alternative route to report. This may be the line manager's manager, HR or an independent whistleblowing hotline.

No retaliation and support

You need to create confidence that people who report in good faith will be supported, and face no retaliation or victimisation as a result. Remember to encourage both victims and witnesses to come forward in confidence.

No reporting doesn't mean no bullying and harassment. It's more likely people aren't sure how committed your organisation is to doing the right thing.

> " *No reporting doesn't mean no bullying and harassment. It's more likely people aren't sure how committed your organisation is to doing the right thing.*

Decision 37: Avoid the line manager lottery

Some policies will indicate that your immediate line manager knows you best and can apply their own discretion to offering flexibility and time off. I like the idea, but at the same time it sounds alarm bells. Line managers have a vast range of experience, and empathy. Some will be confident applying discretion and being fair in their approach across the team. Others will be less confident or capable. Perhaps they were promoted for their exceptional technical skill and managing people is not a natural strength.

And I've lost count of the times managers expect to read a policy and find instructions for exactly what they should do in any specific circumstance they need to handle. It's not realistic because life and people are complex.

So, how do you find the right balance? Consider including line manager guidance in policies to direct them where to seek advice if they're unsure. And provide employee guidance about how to get support when it feels like those discretionary decisions aren't fair or right. Don't rely on the manager or employee knowing who to go to.

Decision 38:
Make information easy to find and understand

You might be wondering whether any new guidance you introduce should become a formal policy or informal guidance. The biggest difference between the two is that a policy might be mandatory, and guidance is more flexible. It doesn't really matter so long as people can find what they need, when they need it, and the information is easy to understand.

Domestic abuse

Since the Covid-19 pandemic, there's been a surge in employers offering support for people suffering from domestic abuse. I fully support it because abuse has such a detrimental effect on your sense of self and productivity (I speak from experience). Work might be the only place you have regular contact outside the home and having support from your employer can make a huge difference when rebuilding your life.

It's no exaggeration to say I've reviewed domestic abuse policies that are nine pages long, prioritise the employer's obligation and bury victim support in appendix B. And there's no mention of wanting perpetrators to stop or how they can access support to help them do that.

If a person is in crisis, this is the information they need to find on page one:

- Guidance to contact the police if their life is in immediate danger
- Signposting to specialist services for victims to escape harm
- Signposting to specialist services for perpetrators to prevent further harm
- Whether you'll fund three nights in a hotel, to help people get out of the immediate cycle (for both victims and perpetrators)
- What support you offer e.g., time off, access to legal advice, therapy etc

I've been asked a few times whether domestic abuse support should be written as a policy or guidance. And my response is to ask a different question. If a person is in crisis, how helpful is your information?

As well as domestic abuse, there are other major life events that people need support with. As you build skill in listening to your employees' mixed life experiences, you'll find out quickly when there are other gaps to fill in your offering.

> " *If a person is in crisis, how helpful is your information?*

Decision 39:
Build based on feedback from your employees

When updating or implementing policies, you can get valuable information from your employees. Ask them to highlight what in your policies is really valued as well as what's lacking.

<u>Trans and transitioning</u>

The LGBT+ network at Sky had initially developed a guide for colleagues going through gender transition at work. It signposted support available and practical advice such as updating a personal profile, email address, ID card etc. The *'Transitioning'* guide was available on the network's intranet page and had been developed in response to feedback from the Workplace Equality Index provided by Stonewall (Europe's largest LGBT rights organisation), who had highlighted that the 'T' in the commitment to LGBT+ needed a louder voice. We agreed.

> " *When updating or implementing policies, build <u>with</u>, not for.*

A little later, the broader trans community at Sky suggested the guide be updated to include information about non-binary people, with guidance on how to be supportive for managers and teams. They also wanted the guide to be easier to find, as people might not go looking on the LGBT+ intranet pages. So, the LGBT+ network and the HR team collaborated to evolve the initial guidance into a policy, so it could be published in the A–Z policy directory. On final review, the trans community pointed out a couple of clumsy descriptions that needed updating, then the new '*Trans and transitioning*' policy was published.

When updating or implementing policies, build <u>with</u>, not for.

Reflection section

Key decision themes

- Many policies don't reflect human kindness.

- Historically workplace policies have been one-size-fits-man.

- To create the possibility of gender equity at work, you must create the possibility for it at home.

- Supporting carers keeps them in your workforce.

- Give people sitting next to each other the same support.

- Use language that normalises including everyone.

- Ensure people feel confident reporting bullying and harassment.

- Don't rely on managers and employees knowing what to do.

- If a person is in crisis, information needs to get straight to the point.

- When updating or implementing policies, build <u>with</u>, not for.

Questions to answer before we move on

- Do your policies reflect the kindness you offer when someone needs support?

- Do you have any policies with length of service exclusions?

- How confident are you that people in your organisation know you're committed to doing the right thing if they need to report bullying or harassment?

Be flexible and religion friendly

Having flexibility at work recognises you as a whole human and accounts for what else is happening in your life. You might need to attend an appointment, take care of a relative, have time off to study, practise faith, pursue hobbies or sports, recover from illness or injury. Or something else.

Times have changed

In the 1920s huge social changes happened when World War 1 saw women flocking to work to take over the jobs of the men who had gone to war.[9] It was the first decade women's abilities outside the home were truly recognised.

Fast forward to today and there's an expectation for women to '*have*' it all and '*do*' it all. As well as having successful careers, women are still most often the people that run the home, organise holidays, update the children's wardrobes, meal plan, cook, clean, manage home renovations, buy the gifts, take care of aging parents, fill out college applications and on it goes.

Many of these demands didn't exist 100 years ago, and I listened to a podcast recently that made me laugh out loud when it described women in the future looking back at this time and asking *what the actual f*ck?!*

While many of us are grateful gender equality continues to improve, we must acknowledge the relentless strain, for working mothers especially, to parent like they have no career, and work like they have no family. Particularly when they're not earning enough money to easily afford help.

So instead of risking burn out, many women are forced to slow down their careers. They avoid promotion, reduce their hours (and are overlooked for promotion because of it), or they leave altogether.

If men are routinely overrepresented at senior levels in your organisation, one of the causes might be that your working patterns and expectations are still designed for people to be able to dedicate almost all their energy to their work. That pattern and expectation only really works if people have someone taking care of everything on the home front, much like in the 19th century. Working mothers seldom have the same support.

> " *We must acknowledge the relentless strain, for working mothers especially, to parent like they have no career, and work like they have no family.*

Decision 40:
Focus on results delivered instead of hours worked

Having the autonomy to choose how and when you work, particularly at a senior level, is becoming an expectation. This is in part due to the Covid-19 pandemic accelerating an appreciation for time spent doing hobbies, with family or recharging in exchange for commuting.

Get the job done

During my corporate career, time spent in the office was about building and maintaining relationships, learning from others, and collaborating. I'd feel my brain slowing down around 3pm, which was usually temporarily fuelled by sweet treats and yet another cup of tea, before deciding to call it a day and head home. Knowing that about myself, I tended to get in early, schedule lots of mini breaks and work from home a couple of days a week to create uninterruptible thinking and delivery time.

On my first day at Sky, my boss told me all about the campus and encouraged me to use the onsite gym, nail salon and table service restaurants at times that suited me. Immediately providing permission to exist as a human. As I echoed that permission to my new team, I told them I didn't mind where they worked, so long as what we needed to deliver got done. And they knew to ask me for help when they needed it. It was totally normal to be in a meeting and see someone with wet hair as they'd just come back from the gym, and to join meetings from anywhere, as most of them were virtual due to team members living in different countries.

When you create a trusting environment for people to choose when and how they deliver, you're supporting them to deliver their best work.

Decision 41:
Move away from the full-time default

Most jobs are designed for full-time workers because of the way headcounts and budgets are allocated. This immediately rules out a large number of people despite them having the skills you need.

Insurance company Zurich saw a leap in the number of senior women applying when they added six words to their job adverts: *part time, job share* and *flexible working*.[10] They reported a 16% rise in women applying for jobs and a near 20% jump in female applications for management roles.

Not everyone wants to work full time
When I left Sky, every head-hunter that approached me about new potential roles had been briefed that the role had to be full time based on the amount of work that needed to be delivered. I knew I wasn't interested in doing another full-time corporate gig, so they missed out on the opportunity to see what impact

I could make in their organisation. The out-of-date approach was another little gentle nudge toward setting up my own business.

<u>Job shares</u>

I love what the organisation *Share My Telly Job (SMTJ)* is doing. They advocate job sharing for freelancers in the TV industry as they realised so many women were having to walk away from jobs they love, because the hours don't accommodate having a career and a family. Before children, freelancers could be flexible, travel and work long hours. After children, they need the industry to provide flexibility in return, but there are virtually no part-time jobs. SMTJ champion job sharing as the most practical solution to this problem.[11] It works by matching up two people with the same skills to work on a show and share the hours between them. So next time you're watching your favourite programme, you might have had the benefit of multiple minds being producer, editor etc. The advantages to the production companies are a *much* bigger pool of talent, a greater mix of creativity, and more authenticity representing women on screen with more women in production roles.

When you translate this into other industries and sectors, another benefit is job sharers can provide year-round continuity, as one of them can be available 52 weeks a year, while the other is on leave.

There are so many people who could benefit from roles that aren't full time, including people who've had long careers and just want to work less now, entrepreneurs who need space to get their start-up off the ground and colleagues who are caring for an elderly parent. The list goes on.

Decision 42:
Resize workloads

Resizing workloads is a skill that needs more development in every organisation I've worked in. Because the people who'd reduced their hours usually ended up underpaid and overworked.

Each time you agree to a reduction in pay for a reduction in hours, you also need to ensure a reduction in workload. For example, if someone moves from working five days a week to four, that represents 20% of the workload to be removed and there are a few options you should consider:

> " *No one's wellbeing or career development should be impacted because they reduce their hours.*

- **Shrink** – Can you shrink the workload by redefining what's essential, automating tasks, or reducing frequency of tasks?

- **Stop** – Can you just stop work that is no longer valuable to customers, or the organisation?

- **Share** – Are you able to review capacity across the team or create a job share?

Prioritise reducing the work, so people working less than full time don't miss out on things such as conferences, training, networking, going to the gym and lunchbreaks. No one's wellbeing or career development should be impacted because they reduce their hours.

Decision 43:
Create options for shift workers

In shift-based environments, options like home working and providing total autonomy for people to choose the hours they work isn't an option. And because people can't provide the same options for everyone and don't want to be unfair, that often becomes an argument for resisting flexible working at all. When you review the definitions for equality, *'treat everyone the same'*, and equity, *'provide people with the same outcomes'*, this argument soon unravels.

The reality is different workers have different things that are suited to the work or environment they're in. Some are provided a vehicle; others need to find their own transport. Some are provided a uniform; others need to wear their own clothes. Some have the option to earn more through overtime; others receive the same salary no matter how many hours they work. You get the idea.

> *Inclusion is the opposite of one-size-fits-all.*

Inclusion is the opposite of one-size-fits-all.

<u>Empower teams to find what works</u>
To create a flexible environment for shift workers, different teams may need and want different things. This is a great opportunity for collaboration, experimentation and failing fast to find what works. You might start with one team, who already have a good idea about what they'd like to achieve and at the same time fully appreciate the operational demands. They have a vested interest in finding solutions and encouraging them to be accountable and use their own judgement will help them do it.

Here's some ideas you can offer the team as they explore:

- **Core working hours** – Which are the hours when demand is at its highest? Can the team agree the rest of the rota between them? Early risers may choose the early mornings and night owls can take the late shift and wake up later.

- **Sliding start and finish times** – Is there an option to alter start and finish times by an hour or two?

- **Split shifts** – Can an eight-hour shift be split 6–10am and 7–11pm? This could help parents with the school run, carers make hospital appointments or pet owners get their daily feeds in.

- **Shift swaps** – Can this be done informally amongst colleagues? With advance notice to schedulers? Or using apps for automation?

- **Accrue additional leave for working unpopular shifts** – Could this work for people who have varying support with family life at different times of the year? Maybe a partner is in the armed forces, or parents who provide childcare spend big chunks of time travelling or living in another country.

I recommend agreeing a three-month trial period and asking the experimenting team to report back on what worked as well as what didn't. You can use those insights to equip other teams to find their own solutions.

Decision 44:
Introduce bank holiday swaps

Bank holidays in the UK are when banks and many other businesses are closed for the day, and like public holidays elsewhere they've become a usual part of the annual holiday allowance for most workers.

Four out of the eight bank holidays in England relate to dates in the Christian calendar. And Scotland and Ireland also have an additional day's holiday to recognise their patron saints, St Andrew and St Patrick respectively.

Your workforce is likely made up of people with a variety of faiths, spiritual and agnostic beliefs. So, instead of restricting people to take the same shared holidays, you can provide the option for people to swap a Christian date for another date that has more meaning to them. For example, swapping two days off at Easter for two days off at Diwali. Spotify, Deloitte and Grant Thornton are among some of the businesses already offering flexible bank holiday dates.[12]

Different options in different teams
The Finance team at Sky were ahead of the game when they introduced holiday swaps many years ago. Colleagues across the department understood the demands of month end, quarter end and year end, and they agreed three or four specific holidays that could be swapped each year. Some colleagues did, many didn't, and it worked.

In the customer-facing teams, they recognised the need to be available to customers 365 days a year, so the eight bank holidays were added to each person's holiday allowance and booked in the same way. A colleague in HR chose that contract because he liked the flexibility to choose which extended family events to take part in during public holidays, and which ones he could avoid by declaring he needed to be at work. I hope I haven't just outed him!

Ramadan
Ramadan is observed by Muslims worldwide as a month of fasting, prayer, reflection and community. Intended to increase self-control and hoping that the good behaviours will become habits in all aspects of life. During Ramadan, most Muslims will wake before dawn for a meal, and end their daily fast at sunset with a feast called Iftar.

Imran was one of the awesome engineers I met working at Sky and he describes Ramadan as taking the luxuries out of life and grounding yourself in what really matters. He shared with me the challenges the usual shift patterns created when you've not eaten for 18 hours and you do a physical job, particularly when Ramadan falls when the weather is warmer. With full support from his leaders, Imran collaborated with the shift scheduling team to provide the option for engineers to work half days or full days during fasting if they wanted to.[13]

A simple fix that made a huge impact.

And in the contact centres, managers would organise Iftar tables for the team to join Muslim colleagues as they broke their fast during the late shifts.

Such a wonderful celebration of the mix of cultures working together.

The end of Ramadan is marked by Eid ul Fitr, a three-day festival to celebrate what you've achieved during the month. Friends and families socialise and exchange gifts (a bit like Christmas), and attendance at a mosque for special prayer is custom on the first day. A wonderful reason to switch a Christian day off for a more meaningful day.

Reflection section

Key decision themes

- Creating a trusting environment for people to choose when and how they deliver supports them to deliver their best work.

- The default of jobs being full time means ruling out large numbers of people, despite them having the skills you need.

- No one's wellbeing or career development should be impacted because they reduce their hours.

- There are many ways to create flexibility for shift workers and they have a vested interest in finding the right approach.

- Give people the option to take public or bank holiday allowances at times that are more meaningful to them.

Questions to answer before we move on

- How much autonomy do office-based staff have with their working hours?

- What percentage of people work part time in your department? (an estimate is ok)

- How easy is it for shift workers to change their hours when they need to?

Shrink pay and benefit gaps

The main area of focus for pay inequity so far has been to look at the differences in pay between women and men. In the UK the *Equal Pay Act* was introduced in 1970, meaning a woman and a man in the same employment, performing the same work, must receive equal pay.

Then in 2017, the British government introduced further legislation – *Gender Pay Gap* reporting.[14] This requires all organisations with 250 or more employees to publicly report their own mean and median pay and bonus gaps, for all women and all men. Before we go any further, I get confused with mean and median, so here's some simple definitions:

- **Mean** – otherwise known as the average, so the sum of all the numbers, divided by the total number of numbers
- **Median** – midpoint of all numbers when stacked highest to lowest

Across the UK the median hourly earnings reported for women and men showed a difference of 27.5% back in 1997, meaning the mid-point for women's salaries was 27.5% lower than the mid-point for men's salaries. The mid-point gap had been steadily reducing and got to 14.9% in 2020, before increasing to 15.4% in 2021.[15] Reports indicate this was due to the increased load society expected women to pick up, when childcare and schools closed during the pandemic. Many reduced their hours or left the workforce altogether. The same expectations weren't typically placed on men.

Now all this is important to understand, and it's great to see pay gaps closing. But at the same time, we need to go beyond gender, and I'm not convinced the way through that is to introduce separated reporting for ethnicity pay gaps, disability pay gaps etc. As, whilst regulatory pay gap reporting helps to shine a light on some of the pay inequities, it's a blunt tool, as it only shows a small slice of the issues.

Decision 45:
Reframe the focus on pay gaps

When you consider socioeconomic status, often measured as a combination of education, income and occupation, you'll find that along with all the people from underrepresented groups who face barriers, there are White men who aren't having a great time in life either. Maybe because they live in an area where education and infrastructure to provide jobs, or transport to get to work, has been underinvested in. But you would never find this by looking at gender and

> " Look at pay gaps with an intersectional lens to reframe the focus and close the advantage gap for every demographic.

ethnicity pay gaps separately. So, you need to look at pay gaps with an intersectional lens to reframe the focus and close the advantage gap for *every* demographic.

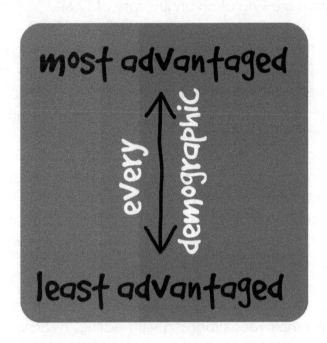

Decision 46:
Provide financial assistance when needed

At the time of writing, here in the UK, there is a cost-of-living crisis, with food and fuel prices surging, meaning many people are struggling to pay for the basics of living. And those who were already battling are being pushed into financial hardship, or worse poverty.

The rise in prices has fuelled the UK inflation rate to a 40-year high, and despite growth in regular pay, the impact on the real value of pay is a drop for most people. That drop is falling faster than any time since comparable records began in 2001.[16] And there's a direct correlation with borrowing on credit cards, which is growing at an annual rate of 12.5%.[17]

Now the answer isn't necessarily to increase wages in line with inflation, as that could fuel inflation further, and lead to a prolonged recession and loss of jobs in the longer term. So, in unprecedented times like these, it's better to increase pay further than you normally would, but not match inflation. And if you can, provide other short-term financial support e.g., discounts, vouchers, one-off cash payments etc. Then, when inflation starts to recede, and if recession sets in, organisations aren't left with salary bills they can't afford. Which would make a recession deeper.

If you don't already know, I urge you to find out if you have employees struggling with eating, heating and housing, and put together a mixed and collaborative response team. Particularly if your organisation is reporting huge profits and the people at the top are still able to take their ever-increasing bonuses.

According to the Office for National Statistics' Business Insights report, more than one in 20 big businesses have given employees a cost-of-living bonus to help with rising costs. For example, major UK retailer John Lewis Partnership (JLP) have provided a one-off cost of living support payment of £500 for employees, are offering free food over the winter, and have doubled their financial assistance fund to help with bills. They also committed £16 million to Britain's pig farmers, and £2 million support and 2.8 million meals to vulnerable communities.[18] In their half-year report, the Chair of JLP said, '*We are forgoing profit by making choices based on the sort of business we are, led by our Purpose – "Working in Partnership for a happier world" – by helping our Partners, customers, communities and suppliers*'.

Indirect assistance

The other things organisations can do, when they haven't got the money to provide direct financial assistance, is consider things like changing start and finish times. This could mean people can travel when train fares are cheaper or pay less often for breakfast clubs and after-school clubs.

There's always something you can do to provide support, and it doesn't have to cost millions.

Decision 47:
Determine your CEO to average worker pay ratio

According to the World Inequality Report, the richest 10% of the global population own 76% of all wealth, and 2020 saw the steepest increase in billionaires' wealth on record. Meanwhile, 100 million people sank into extreme poverty.[19]

The Economic Policy Institute found that while millions were jobless due to the pandemic-driven recession, US CEO pay soared nearly 19% in 2020.[20] On average their incomes were 351 times as much as their typical worker, up from 307 times as much in 2019, and only 21 times in 1965.

Overpaid CEOs is not new news. In 1997 the late Peter F. Drucker, an Austrian American management consultant whose work has contributed to the philosophical and practical foundations of modern business, suggested the pay ratio between CEOs and employees be a maximum of 25 times as much. And in 2001 he reduced the recommendation to 20 times as much.[21]

Solving the problems of humanity

In 2015, the CEO at Gravity Payments went even further. They raised the salary of everyone at the Seattle-based credit card processing company to at least $70,000 a year.[22] The CEO took a million-dollar pay cut and downsized their lifestyle because, as they say on their LinkedIn profile, '*I want to be a small part of a revolution where business ceases to be primarily about money, but instead is focused on mission, service, and solving the problems of humanity*'.

The critics predicted bankruptcy, but that didn't happen. Some employees had their salary double overnight, and it meant they could afford to buy their first home, start a family, or make another life ambition come true. This led to staff turnover significantly reducing, fiercely loyal employees, and the company retaining the collective knowledge of how to help their customers. Gravity Payments has since doubled the number of employees and tripled the size of the business.

Perhaps employers should be required to report their CEO to average worker pay ratios.

Decision 48:
Pay a real living wage

Salaries affect the productivity and quality of life of your work force. When you have enough money to live safely, you have a roof over your head, less stress in relationships, more stability bringing up children and better physical and mental health.

You don't need to wait for the government to solve every problem, you can choose to go beyond mandated minimum wages and pay salaries that meet the cost of living.

In the UK, the Living Wage Foundation has accredited over 11,000 employers, who are paying the real living wage directly to employed staff and regular third-party contracted staff, such as cleaners, security, or catering.[23] The campaign

> " People contributing to the success of your organisation should receive enough money to live on.

for real living wages began in 2001, when Citizens UK brought together low-paid workers living in east London. Many were juggling two or three low-paid jobs, and still didn't earn enough money to live on.

Since then, hundreds of thousands of employees have received a pay rise and the Living Wage Foundation independently calculates an hourly rate and announces it each November.

People contributing to the success of your organisation should receive enough money to live on.

Decision 49:
Monitor independent pay decisions

It's not just the gaps between the highest and lowest paid that need reviewing, it's also the pay gaps between similar job types.

The next page has an (oversimplified) illustration with two employees: a woman called Simi and a man called Taylor. They start their career with same level of experience and skill. They accept roles in different teams, with different hiring managers, and Simi starts on £30,000 a year, and Taylor on £31,500.

Simi and Taylor both work for the company for 10 years, they each get a 3% annual pay increase (rounded to the nearest pound) as standard, and they're promoted every three years, receiving a 10% increase in those years. Simi continues to earn less each year. After 10 years, Simi's cumulative income totals £424,009, and Taylor's £445,207. The initial £1,500 salary gap becomes a cumulative income gap of £21,198.

Year	Pay increase	Simi's salary	Taylor's salary
0	-	£30,000	£31,500
1	3%	£30,900	£32,445
2	3%	£31,827	£33,418
3	10% (promotion)	£35,010	£36,760
4	3%	£36,060	£37,863
5	3%	£37,142	£38,999
6	10% (promotion)	£40,856	£42,899
7	3%	£42,082	£44,186
8	3%	£43,344	£45,511
9	10% (promotion)	£47,679	£50,062
10	3%	£49,109	£51,564
	10-year total	**£424,009**	**£445,207**

If they continue this same rolling pattern of 3%/3%/10%, after 20 years the cumulative gap becomes £54,069, and **after 30 years it's £109,323**, which means you've paid Simi significantly less. You can apply the same logic for bonus payments and pension contributions.

When you ask yourself if that feels right, your likely answer is no. And when you look at which demographics in your organisation are disadvantaged in this way, you'll find this is a more common experience for women and people from underrepresented groups. While we're on this topic, I'd like to address the suggestion that women should be better at negotiating their starting salary, as men tend to get a better deal. This puts the weight of fixing the problem on the people who are being disadvantaged. Don't do that. Instead, make sure you carry out an annual pay review and put right any inequities.

Did the organisation or managers pay Simi less because they're fundamentally bad and deliberately wanted to create economic inequity? No, but there should be a process to calibrate Simi and Taylor's salaries.

Independent decisions are made all the time and that's ok. At least once a year you need to take a step back and look at the outcomes of those decisions, and issue backdated payments for any loss of earning.

Here are some questions to ask to make sure independent decisions aren't unfairly impacting a particular group:

1. **Have there been any independent pay decision penalties?** – Have people who've joined in the last year been given different salaries for the same role and responsibilities?

2. **Are there any part-time penalties?** – Are pay increases lower for people who work part time? Have they maintained high performance within the hours agreed, but been penalised because they contribute less than someone working full time?

3. **Are there any parenthood penalties?** – Are people getting paid less after they've had

children? Do the penalties increase if they have more than one child?

4. **Are there any proximity penalties?** – Is there a correlation with lower pay rises for people who work remotely or come into the office less often?

5. **Who are the most disadvantaged?** – Which demographics have the biggest pay gaps? Is there a greater disadvantage when you overlap multiple characteristics e.g., part-time women who are parents?

You might find everything looks great and feel reassured, or you might find areas of concern that need your attention.

Either way, it's better to know.

Decision 50:
Provide benefits that match life circumstances

Many organisations offer a wide range of benefits including high street discounts, dentalcare, healthcare, bicycles, gym membership, health insurance, apps to track wellbeing, and more. The offering can be so vast and learning about each offering is like reading an encyclopaedia, so people juggling busy lives just don't have the capacity to absorb it.

When you look at your benefits uptake, you often find they aren't being utilised by the people who would benefit the most. For example, some private healthcare policies don't cover support for menopause (experienced by half the population), yet they do cover erectile dysfunction!

Good practice here is to continuously review and revise your benefits offering and invite feedback from the people you're offering them to. And make sure the research group represents a diverse mix including age, because what you want and need at 20 may look very different at 40 and again at 60.

Decision 51:
Recognise your rocks and rockstars

I've seen a lot of recognition awards and spot bonuses that celebrate high-profile work where the person worked long hours, pulled off the impossible and nearly had a nervous breakdown whilst doing it. Ok, I might be exaggerating but stay with me. When this happens, the people having a nervous breakdown, and all the people who kept everything else going while they did that work, receive the message that high-pressure delivery is what's most important to this organisation. What about stability? What about excellent customer service?

If this scenario sounds familiar, I encourage you to focus on the rocks (people who maintain everything) as well as the rockstars (people doing shiny high-profile work).

Next up, consider how people get nominated for those awards and ultimately who picks the winners.

You might guess what's coming here. Create a clear set of guidelines with an *inclusion reminder* (Decision 11) to make sure you have a diverse committee. And that committee must review the diversity of the people they've shortlisted before making the final decision.

Decision 52: Repurpose long-service awards

When so many workers today anticipate having multiple careers throughout their lifetime, I consider this particular tool for retention out of date. Do you really want to gift £200 to Marvin in accounts, who's been there 20 years and refuses to adopt the systems introduced 12 years ago, over Carolyn who joined eight months ago and introduced some formulas that turned a four-day job into a 12-minute task?

Instant recognition

I encourage you to repurpose (frankly expensive) long-service awards, and in their place provide an instant peer-to-peer recognition programme so colleagues can thank each other as good things happen. It's much more meaningful and can be a great way to bring your values to life in real time.

I've seen versions where colleagues have unlimited nominations with no monetary value attached, then each quarter there's a selection process to give out monetary awards. If you adopt this approach, make sure there's an *inclusion reminder* for a diverse committee to review the diversity of winners before making the final decision.

You can still send a card for service anniversaries if this is something important to people in your organisation. Just don't make it a financial benefit.

Hidden long-service awards

You might also find things like increased holiday entitlements are linked to longer length of service. And again, I'd encourage you to repurpose anything that recognises length of service toward recognising everyday contribution.

Decision 53:
Reflect people, planet and profits in your bonus structure

I've lost count of the number of organisations who report bold ambitions for inclusion, but there's no EDI objective in the executive bonus structure. Most structure executive bonuses around financial performance and have yet to connect the responsibility for social and environmental action.

" *A bonus structure that doesn't account for impact on people and planet makes whatever you're saying about inclusion and the environment in your corporate narrative look like pretty wallpaper that can be torn down at any moment.*

In today's world, leaders lead more than a business, they lead people and are responsible for the impact made on the world. To support your inclusion vision, environmental, social and governance (ESG) commitments and organisation purpose, your leadership compensation strategy needs to drive all ambitions.

Think people + planet + profit.

This approach will nudge leaders to make fairer decisions about things like which people's careers they'll invest in, the diversity of suppliers they engage with, environmental impact etc., alongside business performance.

A bonus structure that doesn't account for impact on people and planet makes whatever you're saying about inclusion and the environment in your corporate narrative look like pretty wallpaper that can be torn down at any moment.

Reflection section

Key decision themes

- Look at pay gaps with an intersectional lens to close the advantage gap for every demographic.

- Financial assistance doesn't have to cost millions.

- Maintain a fair ratio for CEO to average worker pay.

- Pay people enough to live on.

- Calibrate independent pay decisions once a year and backdate any loss of earnings.

- Review and revise your benefits offering with the people you're offering them to.

- Form diverse committees when deciding who wins recognition awards.

- Recognise day-to-day impact over length of service.

- Think people + planet + profit in your bonus structure.

Questions to answer before we move on

- How confiden.t are you that the wages you pay are covering the cost of living for your lowest paid workers?

■ What pay gap analysis does your organisation do? Could it be more sophisticated?

■ When you think about the people who get the most recognition in your organisation, how much diversity is there?

Part 5

How to address overrepresentation

Now let's focus on how you build diverse teams. Part 5 looks at: identifying the underrepresented groups you most need to attract, your approach to hiring, and how you can boost career progression, as well as the all-important boardroom diversity.

Be specific about who you want to attract

Increasing workforce diversity is obviously an important part of the role for hiring managers and recruiters. And it's where many organisations focus first. I caution you against jumping straight to recruitment without first building an inclusive culture though, because your diverse hires won't stay very long if the environment isn't right.

> " If you're failing to retain women and people from underrepresented groups, any investment on recruitment will be a bit like pouring water into a leaky bucket.

If you're failing to retain women and people from underrepresented groups, any investment on recruitment will be a bit like pouring water into a leaky bucket.

Decision 54:
Focus on building collective intelligence

I love the way British journalist, author, broadcaster and former table tennis player Matthew Syed talks about diversity in his book *Rebel Ideas*. He describes diversity as a basic ingredient of collective intelligence. And walks through lessons where super-smart people got things wrong, including in the US Central Intelligence Agency (CIA), the UK's Scientific Advisory Group for Emergencies (SAGE), and mountaineers summiting

Everest. They got it wrong because they shared similar academic profiles, career experiences and thinking styles, so they overlooked perspectives that weren't already familiar.

You might have learnt that the best way to filter through CVs was to look at education and industry experience. That creates a very narrow definition of success and makes the gate into your organisation a tight squeeze.

Designing diverse teams is about valuing the skills and experiences of the people you already have in your team. Then taking the opportunity to look for candidates who will bring something new.

Contextual recruitment

Contextual recruitment considers the postcode and family people were born into and relates that to their academic achievements.

Here we have two candidates you're considering for an entry-level role in your legal team:

	College results	Work experience	University
Rebecca	AAA	In a law firm	2:1 (second-class degree) at a university that is considered high status
Ash	BBB	Not in a law firm	1st (highest class honours you can achieve) at a university that is well considered but not high status

If you skim through a pile of CVs and use a traditional method of grades and type of university to make your selection, you'll likely choose Rebecca over Ash.

Let's find out more about them.

	College's average results	Area they grew up in
Rebecca	A*A*A*	Neighbourhood one of the least deprived in the country
Ash	DDD	Neighbourhood one of the most deprived in the country

Now we can see that Rebecca's college grades were actually below the (high) triple A star average of her peers. Whereas Ash is an overachiever, relative to his peers and the context in which he was educated.

With this context, you would be wise to invite both candidates for interview.

Now you won't always find this context on a CV, but next time you're shortlisting, focus on what people have achieved, instead of their grades and where they studied (if they studied at all).

> ❝Focus on what people have achieved, instead of their grades and where they studied (if they studied at all).

Social inequalities
A great way to generate a conversation about this is the 'Social Inequalities Explained in a $100 Race' video on YouTube.[1] During the race,

you see the teacher read out positive statements about life circumstances and for each statement the students relate to, they take two steps forward. Statements include having parents that are married, access to private education, and never worrying about helping parents pay for bills.

When the teacher has finished reading out the statements, the students are all at different start points. The teacher describes this as the 'race called life' and acknowledges that the people at the front have a better opportunity and head start, which has nothing to do with their talent or effort. And if the people at the back had started at the same position, they'd likely win.

> " *Building diverse teams is nothing to do with lowering the bar, it's usually entirely about widening the gate.*

Building diverse teams is nothing to do with lowering the bar, it's usually entirely about widening the gate.

Decision 55:
Make work experience affordable for everyone

When you look back at Rebecca and Ash's work experience and life context, it's possible Rebecca had more opportunity to get work placements relevant to her ambition. Perhaps through her academic network, her parents' network and access to relevant organisations nearby.

If you're in the position to offer work experience, consider whether your organisation is actively reaching those overachievers in underinvested-in areas.

Be open about the support you offer and consider funding for travel, clothing, lunch and accommodation, so personal finance isn't a barrier, and everyone has the same opportunity.

Remove advantage

You may have a legacy of directors finding work placements for friends and family without them having to go through the usual selection process and then expecting them to have the red-carpet treatment. This puts pressure on the hosting team to avoid any negative feedback going back to the director, it doesn't create a typical experience of work, and frankly it's unfair for people who lost out on a place because of the director's demands.

If this is happening in your organisation, I recommend you stop it. Instead, direct all potential work placement candidates to go through your selection process. And if directors are adamant about bypassing the selection process, you could create an offsetting rule; for every work placement they insist on giving to their privileged contacts, they fund another two opportunities for people without that same advantage.

Decision 56:
Know the difference between positive discrimination and positive action

These two concepts get mixed up and it's worth knowing the difference.

Positive discrimination is hiring someone because of a demographic characteristic they have, but they don't have the necessary skill and experience to do the job. It's illegal in the UK and few people want to be hired on those grounds.

A common microaggression is calling someone a *'diversity hire'*. It implies you don't believe they're good enough and they were only hired because of their demographic characteristic. Be warned about Googling *'diversity hire'* as there are plenty of sarcastic memes. Here's one that stands out:

> If we're calling people 'diversity hires' then I would also like to coin the term 'homogeneity hire': a person who is hired, not because they were the best, but because they were the same. Used in a sentence: 'Mike hired another Mike – he's probably a homogeneity hire'.

Positive action is taking steps to attract people from groups who are underrepresented in your workforce and helping them develop the skills and experience they need to be successfully recruited into your organisation. This is good, and entirely legal, as you're levelling the playing field so more applicants can compete fairly. Below are some examples of things you could do to target people from underrepresented groups.

- **Meet the team sessions**: Invite people to come and learn about your organisation and the jobs you regularly recruit into.
- **Returner programmes**: Provide paid placements for people who've been out of the workforce for a while.
- **Trainee programmes**: Provide paid placements to learn the basics of the job with the support of a mentor.
- **Evening classes**: Invite people to learn new skills that are required for roles you're hiring into. They can stay in their existing jobs while considering a career change.

These examples can range from an hour through to a few months, and it's a good idea to partner with schools, colleges, universities, charities, or community organisations that attract a more diverse mix than you do.

Find more detailed examples of positive action in Decision 58.

Decision 57:
Set specific targets for each department

In every organisation I've worked for and with, there's real commitment to attract people from underrepresented groups. Trouble is the commitments are scattered and their efforts aren't adding up to a more diverse workforce. Warner Media's '2020–2021 *Equity and Inclusion report*' has a great phrase to describe going beyond individual people doing isolated activity: *'We don't believe in random acts of diversity'*.[2]

To achieve diversity, you need to be clear about which demographics you want to attract, redesign your approach and equip hiring managers to make it happen.

Start with your organisation's overall ambition and be specific about the percentage representation you need different demographic groups to have for your workforce to better reflect your community and customer base. Then break those targets down by department. It's not to say every department needs to attract (and retain) the same demographics. For example, you may want to attract more women into Technology, more Black and Brown people into HR, Finance and Marketing, and more people with disabilities into Business Development etc.

When looking at what's achievable, you'll need to consider hiring frequency and regional location. Let's say a manufacturing site only hires three people every six months, and they're based in a community that has a 90% White population. You can't expect their ethnic diversity to shift quickly.

Report on diversity at every level (Decision 27) to define your focus areas and report on the recruitment process (Decision 28) to understand whether it's your recruiters or hiring managers who need the most support. Then design the interventions you need to achieve your goals.

> " *Every team needs to know what their goal is for addressing overrepresentation and how they can make it happen.*

Every team needs to know what their goal is for addressing overrepresentation and how they can make it happen.

Decision 58:
Invite people to 'try before you apply' experiences

Of all the things I've seen, providing *'try before you apply'* experiences is one of the most powerful ways to get fast results. And I have a regulator to thank for this insight.

Regulator-driven insight

The Office of Communications (Ofcom) is a government-approved regulatory and competition authority for the broadcasting, telecommunications and postal industries of the United Kingdom.

In 2017, Ofcom's then CEO Sharon White introduced a requirement for every company holding a broadcast licence to report annually on diversity, as broadcasting is one of the many industries dominated by White middle-class men, working in London.[3] And because broadcast teams made up a third of Sky's workforce, we got involved.

In the first year, we all provided the demographic breakdown of our broadcast teams to Ofcom so they could generate an overall view of the industry. In the second year, Ofcom asked the UK's largest broadcasters to also describe what they were doing to increase diversity, as they wanted to share successes as a potential path for the smaller broadcasters to follow. We all provided a list of initiatives and maybe even felt proud of those lists... but the demographic data showed no significant shifts in diversity from the previous year.

In the third year Ofcom made the genius move of asking the biggest broadcasters to now detail how they were measuring the impact of their initiatives. Anyone working alongside me during this time will remember I was grumpy for about three weeks. Not because I didn't see the value, I really did! It was because we didn't have a consistent way to measure impact. All our initiative owners had their own measures and tying it all together felt like an impossible task.

We had over 30 initiatives across the company with brilliant people behind each one, each with their own story or personal motivation. Many initiatives offered work experience of just a few weeks' support to a tiny number of people. But that support didn't translate into those people getting full-time jobs, so had no impact on our overall diversity. This highlighted a disconnect between effort and sustainable results. Not because people weren't passionate about creating opportunity, but because the initiatives were *random acts of diversity*.

The aha moment

The big aha moment for me came when I found clear evidence of three initiatives that were getting real results year on year. The thing they all had in common was they were very clear about which underrepresented group they were targeting. And the '*try before you apply*' initiatives deliberately pipelined participants into the recruitment processes for permanent vacancies that required those skills.

The three programmes were:

1. **Women in Tech evening course**[4]

   A 12-week programme providing the core skills needed to transfer into a career in tech. The women who participated in these programmes, and got to know the team at Sky, were much more likely to apply and be successful when full-time roles opened up. The tech teams saw a steady increase in the number of women joining and staying in their teams and were nearly at their target of 30% women by the time I left.

2. **Women in Home Service Trainee Programme**[5]
   This was a full-time trainee position lasting several months. Women outside Sky could come and get paid to try out a new role as a Home Service engineer. And women already at Sky had the freedom to try it out and go back to their existing role if they decided it wasn't for them.

   The Home Service team had already tried putting women in their job adverts and making sure language was gender neutral, but it hadn't worked. The team was still only 2% female.

   Engineers at Sky would visit customers' homes, install satellite dishes, set-top boxes and Wi-Fi extenders. There was a perception that women weren't applying because they were concerned about going into customers' homes on their own or wouldn't know how to install the equipment. A new female director for this part of the business wanted to bust any myths. She knew over 70% of domestic spending is made by women, and women were often in the homes when engineers turned up, so having a female engineer arrive would often be very welcome.

   The programme provided all the usual safety training including where the pivot points are on ladders to be able to lift them, and to make sure your van is parked facing the direction of a quick getaway should you be intimidated by a customer. The men were taught this too and always had been.

The team invested time, money and energy into this programme, and they actively encouraged the women who enjoyed the training to apply for permanent vacancies when they became available. As a result, the workforce went from 2% women to 11% in just 18 months!

3. **Early Careers partnerships and insight sessions**[6]
   Sky receives thousands of applications each year for work experience, apprenticeships and graduate programmes. And the data showed a similar demographic profile of applications and successful candidates each time.

   So, the Early Careers team repurposed their budget to visit new schools, colleges and universities that had a wider demographic mix. They brought the Sky experience to those campuses, revamped the website to directly appeal to more diverse young people, and invited students to meet the teams virtually or in person ahead of the application window opening.

   The results were instant.

   Students from all the usual places continued to apply and a whole load of students from these new more diverse schools and universities did too. We made the *gate wider* for students who hadn't previously considered Sky as a place to work. And the increase in women and people from underrepresented groups applying and being successful was huge!

Examples two and three represented high-volume areas of recruitment so not only did the teams see big demographic shifts, those shifts contributed to an overall shift on the demographics of the organisation too.

My three weeks of grumpiness transformed into insight about what really worked, and I was delighted. That insight meant I could confidently provide direction for teams motivated to address overrepresentation.

My message wasn't to cancel all the initiatives that weren't getting big results because many of them were tied to long-lasting relationships that had other value. Instead, the message was to only continue doing them, knowing they're not creating sustainable change, and to direct any further investment into '*try before you apply*' experiences for roles the teams were regularly recruiting into.

That insight led to more teams getting better results faster.

Decision 59:
Provide consistent guidance for hiring managers

Some managers hire all the time, and some only once in three years. No matter which it is, you need to provide them with consistent guidance, so they can be aware of their biases and how to limit them.

Your guidance will provide everyone with a shared narrative about how building a diverse mix into each team helps you better serve your customers or service users.

Include information about bias to help hiring managers understand that every time they make a decision, their social background, life experiences and personal and cultural values influence their reasoning. Which can result in them inadvertently favouring candidates a bit like themselves or the rest of the team (affinity bias) at the expense of others, irrespective of their ability to do the job.

You should share your organisation's inclusion goals, departmental targets and a step-by-step process to create an inclusive job advert (see Decision 60). And if needed, you can add some frequently asked questions to respond to any worries, for example:

Q - Does our commitment to inclusion mean we're excluding White men and can't hire them anymore?
A – No. Our commitment to inclusion is about everyone, and that means we go out of our way

to find a diverse mix of candidates, then select people for their skills and potential based on the criteria in the job advert. We always want to hire the best person for the job.

Q - Isn't it discrimination to hire for diversity?
A - It is illegal to hire someone purely for their personal demographics and not their skills and potential, and our organisation would fail if we did that.

What we're doing is creating a wider mix of applicants to interview. For example, we don't accept interview shortlists of 100% women, as that would mean men never got the opportunity to be considered.

You might find pockets of your organisation that are leading the way with inclusive recruitment, and I recommend collaborating with those hiring managers to create your guidance. Then test it with managers who hire less often to check it's useful.

Reflection section

Key decision themes
- Designing diverse teams is about valuing the skills and experiences of the people you already have. Then taking the opportunity to look for candidates who will bring something new.

- If you're in the position to offer work experience for young people, consider whether your organisation is actively reaching overachievers in underinvested-in areas.

- Positive action is a good thing. Positive discrimination is illegal.

- Every team needs to know what their goal is for addressing overrepresentation and how they can make it happen.

- Initiatives fuelled by passion and energy won't increase diversity if they're not creating a pipeline into real roles you're recruiting for.

- Hiring managers need consistent guidance, so they can be aware of their biases and how to limit them.

Questions to answer before we move on

- What do you look for when reviewing a CV?

- How much similarity in skills and experience do your team share?

- Which area of your organisation recruits most often?

Update your approach to hiring

Recruiters often get a hard time when it comes to finding a diverse mix of candidates, with the expectation it's all down to them, and if they were doing a better job the organisation would be more diverse.

Not true.

Recruiters and hiring managers need to work together to remove barriers, and appeal to a wider mix of talented people.

Decision 60:
Redesign job adverts

There's often time pressure when filling a vacancy, as the team still need to deliver. So, the job advert used last time is tweaked and posted in a rush.

But every time you advertise a role is an opportunity to pause and consider how you might boost the diversity of the team. The following guidance helps hiring managers do this each time they create a job advert:

1. **Look at the team you already have** and what skills and experience you have plenty of.

2. **Identify new skills and experiences** that would make your team stronger.

3. **Write a list of every essential and desirable quality** you'd like a person to have. Put them in priority order and cross out anything you can teach in the first few weeks or months.

4. **Detail the top 3–5 things you need** to help a greater mix of candidates decide whether to apply and make shortlisting easier for you.

5. **Ditch education requirements** or at least set them as low as possible. There are multiple ways to learn, and not everyone chooses, or has the wealth, to go to university.

6. **Restrict industry-specific experience require- ments** as many skills are transferable across industries. And if the whole industry isn't diverse, sticking within the industry is going to make it harder to diversify your team.

7. **Advertise the salary range** to be transparent about what you will pay for the skills you are looking for. A *'competitive salary'* isn't competitive if it's offering you less than your skills can attract. Salary is usually the first thing candidates look for and being transparent saves everyone time. When you're not sure what level of experience you want to hire for, advertise two jobs with two salary bands that distinguish the experience required for each band.

8. **Be specific about flexible working** e.g., by describing the options for choosing or swapping

shifts, or where people can work and how flexible the working week is. If people have secured a working pattern that integrates well into the rest of their life, they're less likely to apply for roles where the options are not made clear.

9. **Describe your approach to criminal convictions** so people know if and when you'll ask. If you don't need to ask (see more in Decision 64), tell people to reassure them. And if you do need to ask, let people know what your approach is. You could say something like this:

If your application is successful, we'll ask you to complete a criminal record check, and depending on the role you've applied for and the nature of any convictions, we might need to withdraw the offer.

10. **Reassure people you'll adjust the process if needed** and let candidates know you'll ask if there's anything they need when you invite them to interview. You might include a sentence like this:

We'll do everything we can to support you during your application and we're happy to make any adjustments to our recruitment process if needed. If you accept an invitation to interview with us, we'll ask you about that then.

(See Decision 68 for examples of adjustments.)

When scanning jobs listed on LinkedIn, you can tell how inclusive the organisation is by how long the list of requirements are. The longer the list of requirements, the less inclusive the organisation is.

> *" The longer the list of requirements, the less inclusive the organisation is.*

Decision 61:
Advertise all vacancies

To create a greater mix of applicants, advertise all roles for at least two weeks before interviewing. You may have a preferred candidate in mind, but unless you're 100% sure their skill and experience are the only option (rarely true), you need to advertise all roles to challenge your automatic (biased) thinking.

If you don't do that people from underrepresented groups will see people from overrepresented groups appointed into career-boosting opportunities that weren't open to everyone. It calls your entire commitment to inclusion into question.

Decision 62:
Make diverse shortlists standard

Requiring diverse shortlists is another opportunity for an *inclusion reminder* (Decision 11) to be built into a standard process.

Your standard criteria could be 50% women, 50% men and no more than 70% White for all leadership positions. For all other positions you might start with no more than 80% of people with demographics that match any area of overrepresentation in the team. You also want to shortlist anyone with a disability who meets your minimum criteria to acknowledge they've likely faced disadvantages in their career so far, and maybe haven't yet had their lucky break.

> *Potential can be an indicator of performance, but performance isn't necessarily an indicator of potential.*

Using standard criteria for shortlisting gives recruiters a clear brief and helps make sure diversity is considered for every vacancy. This may take a bit longer as it will mean looking beyond your usual places, and it's most successful when you've redesigned your job adverts (Decision 60) to appeal to a broader mix of people.

When reviewing the shortlist, focus on the fresh skills and perspectives someone can bring to your team. And remember there's a difference between performance and potential. Potential can be an indicator of performance, but performance isn't necessarily an indicator of potential.

Decision 63:
Restructure your 'Recommend a Friend' scheme

The people in your immediate network tend to be a bit like you. So, if you've got a 'recommend a friend' scheme that provides a reward for introducing people that join the organisation, it's worth reviewing it. Look at the demographic data for recommendations made over the last 12 months to quickly reveal whether it's helping or hindering your diversity goals.

To update the scheme, highlight the areas of your business where people from particular demographic groups are overrepresented and be specific about what sort of recommendations you'd like, for example:

We need more:

- Women in technology, engineering, broadcast and operations
- People with rich cultural heritage in legal, communications and marketing
- LGBT+ people and people living with disabilities in business development, research and governance
- People over 40, and people practising faith in estates planning, customer service and community outreach
- Men in HR

This approach reminds people of your commitment to inclusion and guides them to make recommendations that will help you achieve your inclusion vision.

Decision 64:
Change the filters in your Applicant Tracking System (ATS)

A study by Harvard Business School and Accenture found a major reason millions of capable candidates are being overlooked. It's because automated hiring platforms screen out applicants who could have been selected for interview had their CVs made it in front of a hiring manager.[7]

When the world of recruitment went online in the 1990s it enabled huge numbers of applications to be made for each role advertised. This was tricky to manage, so employers turned to ATS systems that use filters to capture those who most closely matched the requirements of the role. Sounds ok until you consider the use of these filters may screen out anyone who didn't go to university, has a gap in their employment history or a criminal record.

The researchers surveyed 8,720 'hidden' workers who are typically screened out by filters. And they found that companies who intentionally seek out these hidden workers are 36% less likely to face talent and skills shortages. Hidden workers outperformed peers on attitude, work ethic, productivity, quality of work, engagement, attendance and innovation, because they were eager to work and less likely than others to quit. IBM has eliminated college degree requirements for many roles, and JPMorgan Chase no longer ask if applicants have a criminal record.

Criminal convictions

We're all born into different life circumstances, and we all make mistakes. When we want to build a better life a job can provide the stability needed to avoid reoffending.

Ban the Box is a UK campaign to increase opportunities for people with convictions to compete for jobs.[8] They hear from people far too often who can't get past the application stage of a recruitment process because they have to tick 'yes' to the question about convictions and are often then immediately filtered out.

Recruit! is a website for employers supporting the fair treatment of people with criminal records and the first principle of their *'Fair Chance Recruitment'* model is *'Consider the need to ask'*.[9] Many employers choose not to ask about criminal records and instead have measures in place to properly support, manage and oversee employees. If your organisation decides you do need to ask about convictions for some roles, *Recruit!* recommend only asking at the point of making a conditional offer.

Multiple ways to define success

I chose not to go to university as I craved independence and wanted to buy my first home as soon as possible, so accruing student debt wasn't an option for me. My brain also loved learning on the job, and I was ambitious. By 23, I was paying a mortgage, leading a large team and running a business unit that had the highest revenue in the company. I was successful and delivered beyond expectation. So, to discover ATS systems were ruling me out, and people like me, for not being good enough strikes me as ridiculous.

To bypass the filters in job applications, I considered listing a university on my CV but putting it in white text so the ATS would detect I'd been to university, but the hiring manager would see the truth because the white text would never show when printed out or emailed. I never did it, and it's only as I write this, I realise I've never landed a job as a result of applying through a system. All the jobs I've had are because a recruiter contacted me, someone in my network recommended me or I targeted people I wanted to work for by doing my own research on LinkedIn (that's how I landed at Sky).

Decision 65:
Make sure your ATS is accessible

If you use an ATS, you want it to be user friendly and compatible with assistive technology such as screen readers that read out what's on screen for people with visual impairments. If upgrading the system isn't an option for you right now, provide an alternative route for applications e.g., by email.

Read more on accessibility in Decision 83.

Decision 66:
Stop asking for salary history

If someone is being un-derpaid, basing their new salary on their previous earnings means you're continuing their disadvantage. The people most likely to be underpaid are women

> *You can assess someone's capability to do a job without knowing whether they've been historically underpaid, appropriately paid or overpaid.*

and people from minority groups. So, unless you remedy this unfairness, you'll be perpetuating the salary gaps your organisation is aiming to close.

You can assess someone's capability to do a job without knowing whether they've been historically underpaid, appropriately paid or overpaid.

Decision 67:
Ask candidates to provide their demographic information

To make sure you have a diverse mix of applicants, people shortlisted, interviewed, then hired, you need to collect demographic data at the application stage of the recruitment process. That data will tell you which teams are doing well and who needs additional support to run a process that's capable of building inclusive teams.

You'll need to explain to candidates why you are asking for this data and how it'll be used. Here is an example of text you could use to introduce that page in the application process:

We believe our workforce should represent the community we serve. To make sure we're living up to our values, we monitor the diversity of the people who apply to work here. We'd love you to provide your demographic information, so we can hold ourselves to account. We promise to keep it private. This data is never shared with hiring managers and is only ever reported anonymously and as part of a group e.g., last month xx% of applicants were living with a disability, or xx% of people shortlisted for interview were men.

Read about reporting on the recruitment process in Decision 28.

Decision 68:
Ask candidates if you need to adjust your process

When inviting people to interview tell them what will happen and ask if you need to provide any adjustments to the process or timings.

Here are some examples:

- A time extension for tests or case studies could make all the difference for someone with dyslexia.

- A parent might need a few days' notice to arrange childcare.

- Someone with Attention Deficit Hyperactivity Disorder (ADHD) might be relieved to bring a fidget toy to help with concentration.

- A candidate with muscular pain might benefit from having a parking space nearby.

Put people at ease
You can also ask candidates if they'd prefer to meet on Zoom, at the office or at a local coffee shop. And if you do meet in a coffee shop, make sure to let people

know that you'll buy the drinks, to limit concerns about affordability.

Candidates know what they need, so it's best to avoid making any assumptions. Just ask the open question and make the necessary adjustments.

Decision 69:
Provide interview questions in advance

One of my clients was initially hesitant about providing candidates with questions upfront. They thought it would mean they had time to embellish their achievements.

So, we discussed how the pressure of an interview can undermine confidence for people who get nervous, appreciate structure, or people who give their best responses when they've had time to reflect.

The initial hesitation quickly turned to enthusiasm, as they acknowledged that some people perform well at interviews and are great at thinking on the spot, but that doesn't necessarily mean they have the best experience or attitude for the role.

Neurodiverse-friendly questions
To be neurodiverse friendly, questions should be direct, one at a time and avoid being hypothetical or abstract.

Decision 70:
Have more than one person make hiring decisions

A diverse range of interviewers gives you a range of perspectives on the skills and potential of each candidate. And it more likely puts candidates at ease, because a woman wouldn't be interviewed by all men, or a young person by people all over the age of 50 etc. To create a mix, you might ask people at different layers of the hierarchy to get involved, which also creates an opportunity to build their skills and experiences.

Avoid the cookie cutter

'*They must be a good culture fit*' is a phrase used a lot when hiring, and it could be limiting your success in addressing overrepresentation. When we break it down, it usually means wanting someone similar to the rest of the team. It's a bit like getting the cookie cutter out to create identical shapes.

The signal you'll be sending to applicants is they'll need to assimilate to the way things are already done, rather than bring their fresh perspective and add unique strength to the existing team.

Build an *inclusion reminder* (Decision 11) into interview guidance to remind people to focus on the top 3–5 things (Decision 60) that would bring new skills and experiences to the team.

Decision 71:
Reflect your commitments in your employer brand

Your employer brand is how you market the unique experience of working for you. It describes your reputation, and the *'give and get'* proposition for employees. As you make progress on embedding inclusion into your organisation, make sure prospective employees can see it.

Candidates do their research

When people search the words *'diversity'* or *'inclusion'* on your website and in your annual report, you can bet this is something important to them when making their decisions about where to work. Those potential candidates are researching how authentic your commitment is, to make sure they join an organisation making a positive impact on the world.

Generation Z, born late 1990s to early 2010s, make up 30% of the world population and are expected to account for 27% of the workforce by 2025.[10] In the HBR article *'Dear CEOs: A Gen Zer's Open Letter to His Future Employers'*, Kahlil Greene, a senior at Yale who served as the first Black student body President, offers unvarnished advice for today's corporate leaders.[11] He says, *'If you're still making the business case for diversity, your company isn't the place for us'*. Gen-Zers grew up in the era of social movements like #BlackLivesMatter and #MeToo. For most of their lives, they've been immersed in fast-paced political discussions on social media, and they want companies to take a stand. The next generation of people joining the workforce are highly motivated to support social progress and want to take on passion projects that do well for society.

> " *Your employer brand must go beyond the illusion of inclusion.*

Your employer brand must go beyond the illusion of inclusion.

Leadership team

Another watch out is the page on your website that profiles your leadership team. It takes around three seconds for prospective candidates to see if you mean what you say. And if their search delivers a gallery of White men, wearing blue shirts with the same haircut, it can be a warning sign to withdraw.

Your careers page

Should showcase the practicalities of the recruitment experience. It's another place to reassure people you'll adjust the process if needed and be transparent about your approach to hiring people with criminal convictions.

You can also highlight the options for flexible working and any progressive policies for parental leave. And if you have networks or provide time off for volunteering, you can share information on that too.

Employee blogs and videos can be a great way to tell stories about working for your organisation and you'll need to check you feature a diverse mix of people representative of who you want to hire. I once found a page dedicated to diversity and inclusion and the only image was of four White people under the age of 25. Whoops! It was quickly updated.

Social media
Is the place to bring your employee experience to life. The power of your staff networks and where you stand on world events that impact the people who work for you, buy your products or use your services can be made real if you use your social media presence wisely.

Brands with high engagement go beyond highly polished corporate messages and use a friendly tone that relates to the things people are most interested in. Go on LinkedIn and look up Innocent Drinks for inspiration from a social media team, and #LifeAtSky to see how employees are empowered to share their experiences without the need for permission.

Reflection section

Key decision themes

- The longer the list of requirements in job adverts, the less inclusive the organisation is.

- Not advertising all roles calls your commitment to inclusion into question.

- Standard criteria for shortlisting gives recruiters a clear brief to consider diversity for each vacancy.

- Your 'Recommend a friend' scheme could be working against you.

- Your ATS might be filtering out people who have the skills and experiences you need.

- You need to provide an alternative way to apply for a role if your ATS isn't accessible.

- If someone is being underpaid, basing their new salary on their previous earnings means you're continuing their disadvantage.

- You need demographic data to see which recruiters and hiring managers need support to run an inclusive process.

- Your recruitment process might not work well for everyone.

- Some people perform well in interviews. Some don't.

- *'They must be a good culture fit'* could be limiting your success in addressing overrepresentation.

- Gen Z are expected to account for 27% of the workforce by 2025 and they want to know what you stand for.

Questions to answer before we move on

- How long are your job adverts?

- When someone searches the words 'diversity' or 'inclusion' on your website, what does it tell you about your commitment to inclusion?

- What can you learn from your candidate diversity data?

Be deliberate about career progression

When it comes to increasing diversity, there tends to be an overemphasis on recruitment and an underemphasis on investing in the people who already work for you.

To see if this is true in your organisation, review promotions for the last 12 or 24 months and see what percentages of people came from over and underrepresented groups. Then break that data down by department to see if any areas are doing better or worse.

Decision 72:
Find out why careers are progressing at different rates

If you find people from overrepresented groups are promoted at a higher rate than people from underrepresented groups, you'll need to investigate to find out why.

Is it the culture?
What does your engagement survey tell you? What feedback have you had from networks? What do your direct reports tell you? Are there 'in' groups and 'out' groups?

Do you have a retention issue?
Do people from underrepresented groups leave at a faster rate than those from overrepresented groups? Why is that happening? Are people expected to conform to a stereotype and are held back when they don't? For example, Black women being labelled angry instead of assertive when they speak up.

Is it your working patterns?
Are there expectations to socialise and network during family time? Are there frequent last-minute meetings that clash with people's other commitments?

Are leaders promoting in their own image?
What is it about the people from overrepresented groups that mean they're getting more promotions? Is it to do with familiarity? Are people promoting people who would do the job just like them?

Is there diversity at each layer until a certain point?
Do you attract a diverse mix of people into junior roles, but they don't progress past a certain point? Why is that? What is each layer of management doing to address this?

These are just some of the questions you could ask, and your investigation may surface others.

Decision 73:
Sponsor the people you want to stay

Sponsoring someone is when you proactively champion their career development. It's a subtle yet significant difference from traditional mentoring, which is when a senior person provides advice, guidance and feedback to someone more junior.

Informal sponsoring

You probably already know the talented people in your business, and if you haven't already you can set up informal meetings to understand their career ambitions. With that information you, as sponsor, can boost their career development. Make deliberate introductions, endorse their work, invite them to high-profile opportunities outside their usual remit and recommend them to people who are developing or building their teams.

Sponsorship programmes

One of the demographic groups we needed to create more career opportunities for at Sky was people from Black or Brown ethnicities. Particularly focused in the corporate functions, broadcast and customer service teams, because the ethnic mix was already good in tech and product development.

The largely White leadership team wanted a way to bring a greater mix of people into meetings where big decisions get made to get a broader range of perspectives. And the historically underinvested-in colleagues wanted to extend their immediate circles of influence and access greater career experiences.

The *'Shadowing & Sponsorship'* programme was born which created a natural *give and get* advantage. Black and Brown participants identified leaders they'd like to be matched with and together they identified at least six meetings they could attend (shadowing). Either during the meeting or after it, participants were invited to share their observations and ideas and ask questions. As the relationship grew, and the leader got a better understanding of their sponsee's motivation and aspiration, they made introductions to other people in the business (sponsorship).

We decided to launch department by department to learn as we went and make the programme better for each new group that joined. We started with the parts of the business that were already having courageous discussions about the different experiences people from underrepresented ethnicities had at work, as reported in their engagement survey results (Decision 26).

The programme was communicated to all colleagues (including White people) at mid to senior levels, but marketed only to the targeted groups by explaining that the programme had been created to specifically improve the experience and development opportunities for people who were BAME [Note: using BAME is ok in this context because it's describing the total group being targeted and not an individual within the group]. It was important for White people to receive the communications, to see the departmental commitment to inclusion. And it also meant Black and Brown people were less likely to be put in a position of explaining why they had an opportunity that White people didn't.

Did it work? No, not consistently. So, I asked for feedback from the BAME people in departments with low sign-up rates. The thing I hadn't appreciated was the strong sense of hierarchy in some teams. Unless people had been encouraged by their line manager to take part, they believed they would be judged for wanting to take time away from the core day job. Knowing this, we implemented dual communications: one to everyone encouraging sign-up, and one for line managers to consider the power of their influence.

Then it got going. That feedback was another lesson I was grateful to learn.

We also invited every participant to a monthly peer meeting. They shared their shadowing experiences, what they'd learnt about the business and how the relationship with the director was going. And when matches hadn't got off to a smooth start, peer-to-peer advice and encouragement kicked in to try another approach in expressing what they'd like to get from the programme, or people switched to another match. It was a great way for me to learn what was working and what could be done to improve it. And the benefit to participants was building their network and extending their awareness about how the different parts of the business operated. The best sessions were when people shared that they'd applied for a role they wouldn't have considered previously, and the rest of the group cheered them on. There were multiple promotions, and the programme was another success story.

> *If you're not sure how to approach something, involve people in the design, get feedback and evolve it as it grows.*

If you're not sure how to approach something, involve people in the design, get feedback and evolve it as it grows.

It doesn't need to be perfect before you get started.

Decision 74:
Segment marketing for career development programmes

You might think making your programmes open to everyone means they're naturally inclusive and I'm here to bust that myth.

I'll bet that if you review the demographics of people on your last three to five development programmes or leadership events, you'll find the diversity could have been much better. By the way, asking HR to disclose everyone's personal information isn't the way to do this review, as that information must be kept secure

(Decision 25). The right way is to provide the list of names and employee identification numbers and ask your reporting team to let you know the demographic percentages for the group.

I recommend reviewing participant diversity for programmes quarterly if you run a lot of them, and at least annually if you don't.

When you find an overrepresentation trend, your next move is to build an *inclusion reminder* (Decision 11) into the guidance when marketing the programmes. Let's say you have space for 50 people. Guidance for your learning and development team might suggest you want 50% of delegates to be women and at least 20% people from underrepresented groups. That will direct the approach to promoting registrations. You can also provide guidance to leaders for submitting nominations. Let's imagine they can nominate four people in a year. Their reminder is to reflect on the mix of who they're nominating and consider anyone they might have overlooked before making their final decision.

Decision 75:
Design 'talent escalators' for internal mobility

It's often easier to diversify recruitment into some parts of your organisation than others. And there are plenty of skills that can be developed to help people from those teams to make a move up and/or across to another team. These are your talent escalators.

Let's say women are overrepresented in your HR team and underrepresented in Operations or Tech. The overlapping skills could be leading a team, setting direction, problem solving and stakeholder management.

Once you know where your opportunity is, you can proactively build in career experiences to get people ready for a cross-functional move.

Some of the most memorable internal moves at Sky were:

- HR Specialist > Scrum Master > Head of Agile Delivery
- Formula 1 Producer > Communications Manager
- Corporate Comms Director > Customer Service Director > Managing Director

When you design talent escalators successfully, you provide a map for employees to help them navigate various, and maybe less obvious, career paths. This can otherwise be tricky in larger or matrixed organisations.

Decision 76:
Build your reserves bench before you have a vacancy

In sports teams you're constantly scouting for up-and-coming talent alongside coaching your current team to compete at their best. You don't wait for an injury, sickness, or resignation before you start to look for someone who can replace your key players.

When Netflix began, they were intentional about mapping all the diverse talent in the industry, building relationships and knowing who they wanted to approach when they had roles to fill. And they've continued to attract and develop great talent. In 2021 they reported 45.0% of senior leaders are women and 22.7% of US leaders are from one or more historically excluded ethnic and/or racial backgrounds.[12]

When you reflect on the leaders you'd love to come and work for you... how diverse is that mix? Perhaps they're people you admire at competitors, people you've met at networking events, or people you're connected to on LinkedIn. If you realise those people are all a bit like you, set yourself a goal to build relationships with at least five new people who have different demographic profiles. You can ask people to make introductions, approach a greater mix of people to talk to at events, and follow new people on LinkedIn.

You don't need to rely purely on recruiters to find people when you have a vacancy. Great leaders and managers proactively seek out and connect with great people they'd like to work with in future.

Reflection section

Key decision themes

- You have a problem if people from under-represented groups aren't progressing at the same rate as people from overrepresented groups.

- Sponsoring is proactively championing someone's career development.

- Making development programmes open to everyone doesn't mean they're inclusive.

- You can build career experiences to get people ready for cross-functional moves.

- Great managers don't rely solely on recruiters to find their next hire.

Questions to answer before we move on

- Does the diversity in your junior roles mirror the diversity in your senior roles?

- How much diversity was there in the last three senior appointments?

- Which talented people from underrepresented groups would you hate to lose?

Diversify the Board of Directors

A Board is a governing body making key decisions about things such as mergers, acquisitions, senior hires, infrastructure, investments and pay. The people are usually a mix of company directors, and non-executive directors (NEDs) who might serve a few days each month.

Women and people from minority groups have been consistently left out of these positions of power. And because decision makers tend to make decisions that reflect their own lived experiences, this perpetuates inequities across society.

Diversity of thought

'Diversity of thought' is often misreferenced as way to satisfy Boards who lack demographic diversity. The idea is that people don't need to look different or identify with an underrepresented group to bring varying and diverse views to the table. There is truth in this, but it's not enough. We need the people making big decisions to

> We need the people making big decisions to reflect the people who will be affected by them. Without demographic diversity, underrepresented groups are consistently misrepresented and disadvantaged.

reflect the people who will be affected by them. Without demographic diversity, underrepresented groups are consistently misrepresented and disadvantaged.

Overrepresentation and targets

The '*Peter problem*' was coined when a jaw-dropping study in 2020 revealed there were more men named Peter working as CEOs in 350 companies on the Financial Times Stock Exchange (FTSE) index, than there were women.[13] The study found over two-thirds of companies didn't have any female executive committee members with profit and loss responsibility, and 15% had entirely male executive committees. Unsurprisingly, the study also found that the companies with more than a third of women on executive committees had net profit margins over 10 times greater than companies with no women.

In 2017, the '*Parker Review*' made a series of recommendations and set a '*One by 2021*' target for all FTSE 100 boards to have at least one director from a minority ethnic background by December 2021. Eighty-nine met that target, and another five have since then, proving the talent exists.[14]

I like this approach to setting targets because searching for, attracting and hiring one person at that level is both achievable and realistic in four years. You might favour a more ambitious target and you won't get much argument from me. However, I caution against targets to move from 2% to 20% in two years without considerable investment to shift your culture, so you can genuinely welcome people that have historically been excluded from your organisation.

Decision 77:
Challenge the status quo for selection criteria

As part of my research into overrepresentation in the boardroom, I attended a webinar hosted by a large consulting firm and was immediately disappointed. The four clients they'd invited to speak were White women who told the audience they'd never experienced bias (erm... we all do?!). They then said the way they'd become NEDs was because someone they knew tapped them on the shoulder and they bypassed the usual selection process. This is the opposite of an inclusive process, and it was apparent those boards were full of White, privileged people who understood little about EDI. I left the call feeling frustrated and made a cup of tea. I'm British, and I own that stereotype.

When it comes to the makeup of the Board, there's understandably a huge emphasis on risk, governance and financial experience with strict criteria from regulators. Next time you need to replace someone, look at who is staying and if 70% meet multiple criteria from regulators, look at how you can increase diversity and welcome a director with alternative career experiences.

When considering the opportunities to address the overrepresentation of White men, you need to account for turnover rate of company directors and the fact NEDs often serve a seven-year or longer term. This means addressing overrepresentation requires long-term thinking, combined with more immediate changes in approach.

Associate board roles

In 2022 Principality Building Society in Wales introduced two non-executive board associate (NEBA) positions to increase their collective intelligence and provide greater development opportunities to people wanting to gain experience for future board positions.[15]

One of the new appointments was the Data Director of the UK's largest online real estate portal and property website. The other a CEO at a housing association that provides affordable homes, support and care for people on lower incomes in London. This makes total sense for a building society that typically provides savings accounts to protect people's money, and with that money, offers mortgages so people can afford to buy property.

This was a consciously inclusive approach to bring greater insight to the future of work and home ownership discussions.

Football fans in the boardroom

In April 2021 a new football *'European Super League'* (ESL) was announced as 12 clubs attempted to break away from the Union of European Football Associations

(UEFA). UEFA is the Europe-wide body that sets the rules and controls competitions. The 12 ESL club owners saw an opportunity to generate more profit by selling broadcasting rights to the matches. But the plan collapsed within days following furious backlash from fans and politicians across Europe. Mostly directed at the proposal that the 12 founding members would automatically qualify for the league forever![16] Many notable footballers and several clubs also voiced their opposition and expressed concerns over the consequences for the game.

One of the founding ESL clubs was Liverpool FC, and following the collapse they introduced a Supporters Board, to provide fans meaningful representation on strategic issues discussed at executive and board levels.[17] The Supporters Board is written into club regulations and is made up of a diverse mix of 10 supporters.[18] This demonstrates they understood they'd got it wrong and have made a real commitment to do better in the future.

Decision 78:
Shift the power dynamic

It's a happy accident that so many of my clients have CEOs and Chairs that are women (read into that what you will). A couple of their reflections really stood out when I facilitated their discovery calls to help them build their inclusion strategies:

CEO 1 'I sometimes think about the women in our most senior roles and if they needed to progress their careers in a traditionally masculine way'.

CEO 2 'The last thing you want to do is create huge division and when I think of the Suffragettes, I wonder if I'd have been right there with them or thinking ooh no, don't rock the boat'.

I also meet many inspirational men and loved hearing from an executive director who said, *'the overrepresented need to surround the underrepresented with support so they can't fail'*. I couldn't agree more, as most diversity emphasis has been put on *'fixing'* the underrepresented, instead of equipping the overrepresented to create an environment where everyone can succeed.

> 'The overrepresented need to surround the underrepresented with support so they can't fail'.

I encourage you to reflect on these questions next time you're in the boardroom:

- Who gets to speak?
- Who gets interrupted?
- What ratio of speaking and listening do people demonstrate?
- Is it safe for everyone to share an idea that isn't yet fully formed?

- Do the long-servers encourage ideas to be explored, or are they quick to join forces and close things down that don't fit with their own reference points?

When people accept an invitation to the boardroom, you need to remove any 'us' and 'them' barriers. Even small things can make a big difference. It could be as simple as making sure guests know who everyone is, where everybody sits or upgrading technology for genuine hybrid meetings. Hybrid doesn't work if remote attendees can only hear one person speaking, or people in the room can't hear when remote colleagues want to contribute.

> *The leaders today need to consider how history will judge their impact on society 100 years from now.*

Much of what we've learnt about being a leader is associated with hierarchy and status. That needs updating for the world we live in now.

The leaders today need to consider how history will judge their impact on society 100 years from now.

Reflection section

Key decision themes

- Addressing the overrepresentation of White men on boards requires long-term thinking, combined with more immediate changes.

- When people accept an invitation to the boardroom, you need to remove any 'us' and 'them' barriers.

Questions to answer before we move on

- How diverse is your Board or most senior group?

- How do the overrepresented directors support the underrepresented directors?

- How welcoming are the Board to guests?

Part 6

How to operate inclusively

M ost of what we've covered so far is focused on what happens internally. Part 6 explores how buildings and technology can be more inclusive for both employees and customers. We'll also explore business development, customer experience, media and marketing, external narrative, supply chain and wider-world impact.

Provide buildings that welcome everyone

Inclusive buildings need to be adaptable and cater for a whole range of physical, cognitive and personal needs. This applies to the workplace as well as buildings that welcome customers or service users.

Decision 79:
Allocate budget for adjustments

'Reasonable adjustment' is a legal term introduced in the UK Equality Act 2010. It describes a duty to make adjustments where working arrangements or physical premises put a disabled person at a substantial disadvantage, compared to someone who isn't disabled. I like this definition because it acknowledges most infrastructure has been designed for one-size-fits-all and recognises people don't make themselves disabled, the environment does.

> **People don't make themselves disabled, the environment does.**

To fix the environment, you need to allocate a budget for adjustments. Sometimes this will be a capital expenditure to improve buildings. But often it will be a lower cost to equip an individual with what they need to function in your building, for example mobility assistance to travel through an airport.

Decision 80:
Go beyond accessibility audits

Accessibility audits do a good job of assessing your buildings for people with physical disabilities. They highlight what's already in place and provide you with actions to take to comply with legislation.

In the UK, service providers are required to comply with the Equality Act 2010, irrespective of size or turnover, and whether the service is paid for or free of charge.[1] There's a legal requirement to make 'reasonable' changes to:

- **Policies** – e.g., excluding assistance dogs from any 'no dogs' policy
- **Buildings** – e.g., making changes to the structure to improve access
- **Available support** – e.g., providing information in an accessible format or providing an induction loop for customers using hearing aids

What's reasonable?
This depends on the cost, potential benefit, resources your organisation has, and how practical the changes are.

A colleague working for one of my clients uses a wheelchair. Let's call her Laney. The office is in a shared building that hasn't been designed with wheelchair users in mind. It took a huge amount of effort to persuade the building owner to make simple adjustments, just so she could access the facilities. One example that

> *Everyone should be able to make their own cup of tea*

stood out was Laney needing to rely on colleagues to make her a cup of tea (which they were very happy to). She couldn't make one herself because the kitchen was designed with surfaces that could only be reached if you're standing. Everyone should be able to make their own cup of tea.

The turning point came when Laney volunteered to meet with the building owner and demonstrate the disadvantages she was experiencing. It shouldn't have needed to get to that. The lesson here is to consider the experiences of people who aren't just like you.

Temporary adjustments
You need to provide for both long-term and temporary impairments, such as injuries, muscular pain and pregnancy. For example, if your usual parking is a long way from the front door, you might reserve a space outside the building or cover the costs of a taxi for people temporarily unable to manage the walk.

Sensory environment
People have a wide range of access needs, including sensory and cognitive. So, making your building accessible goes beyond making sure someone in a wheelchair can move around and use your facilities.

Another client moved into a beautiful new office in 2022 and they involved colleagues in the design, as they wanted to make sure the building worked for the people using it. The meeting rooms have multi-height boardroom tables, chairs with individual tabletops, and a range of chairs around meeting tables so people can choose one that suits them. They also considered the acoustics and colour palettes so that the environment wouldn't be a sensory overload for some neurodiverse people.

It feels like a building designed by people, for people.

Decision 81:
Signpost trans-inclusive toilets

It's pretty standard to make sure you have toilets that cater for women, men and people who need mobility assistance. It's also becoming much more the norm to provide for people who are trans. Yay!

Without clear provision, those traditional symbols of a woman wearing a dress, a man wearing trousers and a person using a wheelchair suggest trans people aren't welcome in your building.

The media sometimes whips up a frenzy that sexual predators will pretend to be trans to access female-only spaces and attack the women they find there. This narrative is deeply problematic. The truth is sexual predators will attack whatever the circumstance. And trans people are some of the most vulnerable and most likely to be victims of, not the perpetrators of, physical violence. Trans people need a place to pee in peace, the same as everyone else.

Here's what I've seen work:

- **Individual toilets with a door and sink** everyone can use like the ones on planes, trains and in your home. I spoke at an event in an immersive, interactive studio to reach people round the world and most of the venue space was dedicated to super-sophisticated equipment. So, the rest of the venue was small with just two individual toilets for the production team and speakers to use. The sign on the door said '*Just wash your hands*'. I love the simplicity. We're all humans, with bodily functions, and when you've got to go, you've got to go.

- **Dual-purpose accessible toilets** for people who need an accessible bathroom and/or don't identify with the traditional genders of female and male.

- **Friendly signage added to gender-separated toilets** that encourages people to use the bathroom most suited e.g., '*You're welcome to use the bathroom that best fits your identity*'.

Decision 82:
Create uninterruptible spaces for faith and lactation

If you employ people or host customers or service users, you'll have people who need to pray, breastfeed or express milk. So, you need to provide spaces that are appropriate and uninterruptible for them to do it. Which means making the first-aid room *'multipurpose'* isn't the right solution. Just imagine how impossible it is to prioritise when someone faints, someone's breasts are leaking and someone is due to pray all at the same time.

Depending on your building, the numbers of people using it and the frequency of people's needs, these spaces can be permanent or temporary. For example, a private meeting room could be booked for personal use at dedicated times. The important thing is you make the space available and tell people how they can use it. Because without making adequate provision, you're effectively ignoring parts of people's lives and creating a lesser experience for them in your buildings.

Modern organisations offer dedicated space to pray with storage for prayer mats and shoes, and mirrors so people who wear headscarves can check their hair is covered. They also provide separate ablution areas for women and men. Ablution is the ritual washing before prayers for Muslims who follow Islamic faith.

If you enjoy sarcastic humour, watch the *'If men breast-fed'* video on YouTube.[2] You'll find men in a luxury breastfeeding lounge, with cookies, a butler to wash and sterilise equipment, fridges that rank them by how much they expressed that day, and men bragging over who has the most

> *No one should have to feed a baby in a toilet or pray on a fire escape.*

powerful breast pump. At the end you see the more usual reality of a woman expressing milk in a cupboard and putting an embarrassed man at ease, when he comes in looking for stationery.

No one should have to feed a baby in a toilet or pray on a fire escape.

Reflection section

Key decision themes

- Physical differences don't disable people, the environment does.

- Inclusive buildings go beyond making sure someone in a wheelchair can move around and use your facilities.

- Provide a place to pee in peace for trans people.

- No one should have to feed a baby in a toilet or pray on a fire escape.

Questions to answer before we move on

- How easy is it for employees to get a reasonable adjustment in your organisation?

- How are your toilets signposted?

- Where do (or would) people pray or breastfeed in your building?

Provide friendly technology

The digital landscape and the devices we use are part of our daily lives. We rely on them for finding information, communicating and accessing services.

Technology, in one form or another, is often the front door to your organisation. And depending on how inclusive your technology is, that door might not be easy to open for everyone.

" Technology, in one form or another, is often the front door to your organisation. And depending on how inclusive your technology is, that door might not be easy to open for everyone.

Decision 83: Make digital services, websites and apps accessible

The Web Content Accessibility Guidelines (WCAG)[3] provide internationally recognised recommendations to make digital services, websites and apps accessible to everyone. So, users with impairments to their vision, hearing, mobility, thinking and understanding can use them too. Making your websites more accessible isn't just a way to serve a larger customer base, it also boosts your search engine optimisation (SEO) and improves your website's organic search rankings.

There are four WCAG principles:

- **Principle 1: Perceivable** – People can recognise and use your service with the senses that are available to them e.g., pages can be navigated by a screen reader, and every feature can be used when text is increased to 200%.

- **Principle 2: Operable** – People can find and use your content, regardless of how they choose to access it e.g., using a keyboard or voice commands.

- **Principle 3: Understandable** – People can understand your content and how the service works e.g., using clear language and meaningful labels.

- **Principle 4: Robust** – Your content can be interpreted reliably by a wide variety of user agents including reasonably outdated browsers and assistive technologies.

Each of the recommendations have testable success criteria to meet three levels of standard: A, AA and AAA. Services in the UK must achieve level AA to meet government accessibility requirements.[4]

Decision 84:
Make internal systems and tools accessible

Your internal systems and tools need to be checked for accessibility regularly. It can be a big job if you've not done this before as there are typically multiple platforms speaking to each other, with multiple people involved including third parties.

I recommend building *inclusion reminders* (Decision 11) for accessibility into your technology decision-making processes. For example, when approaching potential new suppliers during your procurement process, or when you're defining project priorities with developers during daily stand-up meetings.

> *Accessibility should be baked in as a minimum requirement to all upgrades and new investments.*

Accessibility should be baked in as a minimum requirement to all upgrades and new investments.

Imagine you hire a Business Development Representative with a fantastic track record for generating new and repeat business. Let's call them Jules. Jules has a visual impairment and on day one, the team discover Jules is prevented from doing the job they're brilliant at because your Customer Relationship Management system hasn't been built with accessibility in mind. In fact, it's been so heavily customised that it's not compatible with Jules's usual and widely available screen reading technology, which would have helped them navigate through the menus and pages of customer information and pricing.

Depending on your inclusion investment to date, the fix may require cash and resources to put it right. In the meantime, can you create a different role that uses

Jules's talents and invite them to be a key stakeholder in user design and testing as you make the necessary changes? Your answer should be yes, and you'd be grateful Jules can help you avoid limiting other people's career choices.

Decision 85:
Modernise employee and customer profiles

Which man do you belong to?
When completing online (or paper) forms of almost any type, the first field you're asked to complete is often '*title*', even when it has nothing to do with the transaction.

The use of Mrs and Miss is an old construct that goes back to a time where banks and lenders required the permission of a woman's husband or father, before agreeing to lend her money. Even when she earned more than them!

- Mr = Master
- Mrs = seek approval from her husband
- Miss = seek approval from her father

That only changed in 1980 here in the UK,[4] and in the workplace, it wasn't until 1990 that independent taxation for women was introduced. Before this, the income of a married woman was added to the income of her husband (because she was his '*property*') and taxed accordingly, meaning she got paid less than unmarried women as she had no tax-free allowance.

My supermarket, energy provider, insurers and many other organisations all insist on communicating to me using a title, because it's a mandatory field on their customer profiles. It irritated me so much, I bought a tiny piece of land and new title for £30 off the internet. So now, when I'm forced to use a title, I'm 'Lady' Catherine (there may have been wine involved in that decision, and it makes me smile every time someone uses it to address me).

Small organisations do it too. The local window cleaner insisted on addressing me as Mrs Garrod, despite years of me asking him to call me Catherine. I admittedly ungracefully snapped one day and told him, the fact he insisted on calling me Mrs implied he believed women

> " Many organisations only ask for first name, last name and the world is still spinning.

couldn't earn their own money or decide how to spend it without a man being involved. He insisted it was the polite and proper way to do business. I countered his argument by pointing out it was disrespectful to ignore a perfectly reasonable request. I had huge respect for him when he knocked on the door and thanked me for pointing it out. We both had a good laugh about it, and he's called me Catherine ever since. Woo-hoo!

So, if your organisation has no legitimate use for titles, you should consider not asking at all, or at least provide the option for customers and employees to leave it blank (i.e., don't make it a mandatory field). Many organisations only ask for first name, last name and the world is still spinning.

The person who receives my reservation for a table in a restaurant has no need-to-know which man I *'belong'* to, and men don't get that same intrusion.

Name changes.

The other process to make sure you have in place is for people who change their names following marriage, divorce and transitioning from the sex they were assigned at birth.

If my name has changed to reflect a big change in my life, having you continue to use my old name is another form of disrespect.

You'll need to check your primary systems and any linked systems to make sure updates flow through to things like communications, log-in details, portals for high street discounts etc. And check any legal requirements to protect finances for transgender people, for example here in the UK His Majesty's Revenue and Customs (HMRC) requires a deed poll certificate (legal document) to process pay and pensions.

Again, depending on your investment to date, the fix may require cash and resources to put it right.

Decision 86:
Provide a hardware menu

The people who need anything other than the standard (one-size-fits-all) hardware equipment usually have to speak up (sometimes repeatedly) to get it.

Workplace

In your workplace, how easy is it for people to access adaptive desktop equipment? If you can provide a basic mouse and keyboard ready for a new hire's first day, you can provide a specialised mouse and keyboard ready for the same day too. That's if you ask people what they need before they start.

Products

I recently had to replace my hairdryer and I've probably had over 10 across my lifetime. They've always come with multiple attachments for different hair types, but the one I got recently was the first one that included an attachment and heat safe settings for multiple hair textures. It warmed my heart as well as my hair!

Security devices

For banking customers, what size have you designed the security code devices you provide to help customers access online banking? How long is the code visible on screen? Does your 81-year-old stepdad with shaking hands have any hope of generating the code and tapping it into his touchscreen mobile, before it expires?

Mine doesn't and thankfully he's married to a wonderful woman (yes that's you Mum), who assists him.

Senior citizens

In your local communities and cities, how long do the elderly and people living with disabilities have to cross the road?

In Singapore the Land Transport Authority has equipped over 1,000 pedestrian crossings with an option to have up to 13 seconds more.[5] To get more time, people with mobility challenges can tap a recognised concession card at the crossings. Marvellous upgrade!

Design and test for multiple needs

The difference in experience created for your users can be significant and improved for everyone by designing and testing for multi needs. Then providing a menu of options for people to select the hardware that's most relevant to them.

Personalisation is key.

Decision 87:
Replace outdated terminology

The inherited language used and documented in technology to describe process, activity, or operation often contains terms with harmful associations. While the origins of those words weren't intended to be demeaning, in today's world they're no longer appropriate.

Manuals

When I worked with the leaders of a global engineering business, we discussed a bank who had worked with industry peers Microsoft and EY to publish a guide called *'Is your tech language racist?'*[6] In it they write,

> 'For so long the tech space has used outdated and inherently problematic words and phrases. Our language reflects who we are and who we want to be, so for Lloyds Banking Group to be a truly inclusive organisation, we needed to change. While change doesn't happen overnight, the Group have been at the forefront of this work at an industry level and a tangible difference can be seen in how we communicate'.

The guide includes the following examples:

Outdated terms	Suggested substitutes
Whitelist/blacklist	Allow, trust or approved list/deny, untrusted or blocked list
Master/slave	Primary/secondary
White hat/black hat	Ethical, authorised or non-malicious/ unethical, unauthorised or malicious
Penetration testing	Ethical hacking, red or blue testing, security assessment
Sanity check	Functional test, confidence check or spot check
Dummy	Beginner, test or draft
Grandfather–father–son	Legacy or primary, secondary, tertiary

When reviewing the words, the discussion led to looking up their engineering manuals and seeing similar problematic language. The conversation initially went from getting all their manuals updated, to a challenge around not being able to because the whole industry uses that language. Then it quickly moved to a discussion about using their influence to get every organisation they worked with to change theirs too. I do love a ripple effect like this.

When you review your own tech (and engineering) terminology, I also suggest you replace *'grooming'*, which is the deliberate manipulation of someone for your own intention. Shudder!

Document inclusion proofing

For users of Microsoft 365 there's a feature to help you when preparing documents in Word. It sits alongside the grammar checker and can be turned on by going to File > Options > Proofing > Writing style: Grammar & Refinements / Settings > Inclusiveness (scroll down) and ticking the relevant boxes.[7]

Once activated, it'll pick up on words like 'mankind' and provide suggestions to change it to 'humankind' or 'humanity'.

Try it, and even better, see if you can get the checker applied for everyone.

Instant messaging Bot

Slack provides an inclusive Bot in the instant messaging app to help teams change the way they talk to each other. The idea came from a team who wanted to use inclusive language, recognised they didn't always remember the inclusive terms and didn't want to check a style guide all the time.[8]

The Bot detects non-inclusive language and provides gentle alternatives for age, family status, ability, gender identity, sexual orientation, race, ethnicity, nationality, substance abuse and passive aggressiveness.

In an example,[9] Alex is typing a message to the team and writes:

Alex: Hey guys, you're killing it!

The Bot picks up on this and responds with a message only visible to Alex:

Inclusive Bot – Hey Alex, seems like some of your message includes some non-inclusive language.

> **Expression:** 'Guys' doesn't include people of all genders
> **Suggestion:** Instead, consider using 'team', 'folks' or 'friends'
>
> **Expression:** 'killing it' can be seen as a violent message

Suggestion: Instead, consider using 'great job!' or 'awesome!'

What a fantastic way to nudge our thinking! At the time of writing the inclusive Bot cost $199 for unlimited users.[10]

Decision 88:
Don't rely on Artificial Intelligence (AI) alone

A couple of years ago, I watched an eye-opening documentary on Netflix called *Coded Bias*. It investigated the bias in algorithms after MIT Media Lab researcher Joy Buolamwini uncovered flaws in facial recognition software that doesn't recognise dark skin. Mathematician, data scientist and author Cathy O'Neil also features in the documentary. Her book *Weapons of Math Destruction* explores how some big data algorithms are increasingly used in ways that reinforce pre-existing inequality across society. It's worth a watch.

Racist AI in authentication

Uber has hit the headlines a few times as dismissed drivers and couriers[11] said their facial recognition software was racially biased. The software used to verify workers were available, was failing to authenticate Black people on the basis their faces didn't match their identification photo. Yet it was clearly them. There didn't appear to be the same limitations to access work for people with lighter skin tones.

In a BBC article[12] James Farrar, the App Drivers & Couriers Union's (ADCU) General Secretary, said that Uber had introduced a flawed facial recognition technology which generates '*unacceptable failure rates when used against a workforce mainly composed of people of colour*'. That same article went on... '*According to "Transport for London" 94% of licensed private hire drivers are Black, Asian and minority ethnic*'.

Sexist AI in the hiring process

Back in 2014, Amazon wanted to automate the hiring process by asking AI to review 100 applicants and select the top five to be hired. But by 2015 they found the new system was favouring male candidates for software developer jobs and other technical posts. Which was because the computer models were trained to vet applicants by observing patterns in resumes submitted to the company over the previous 10-year period. Most of which came from men. This reflects the male overrepresentation across the tech industry, and the algorithm interpreted male dominance as a factor of likely success. Amazon initially edited the programmes but ultimately stopped the experiment because although Amazon is at the forefront of AI technology, they couldn't find a way to make its algorithm gender neutral. We can be grateful for this case study on the limitations of machine learning.[13]

The lesson I've taken is, AI learns from what it gets given. And unless the people feeding the machines have been very deliberate about providing unbiased data sets, the algorithms will learn to automate human bias and amplify it. If tech giants Uber and Amazon can't debias their programmes, you should be extremely wary of anyone else saying their product is free from bias.

Reflection section

Key decision themes

- Making websites accessible serves a larger customer base, boosts SEO and improves organic search rankings.

- Accessibility should be baked in as a minimum requirement to all systems and tools upgrades and investments.

- Stop asking women which man they 'belong' to.

- The user experience can be significantly improved for everyone when you design and test for people with different needs.

- Some of the language in your manuals may need updating, as it's no longer appropriate in today's world.

- Be wary of anyone saying their products are free from bias.

Questions to answer before we move on

- How accessible are your external website and internal intranet pages or social channels?

- What terminology do you use to categorise a website that represents a threat?

- What parts of your business use AI? Or are considering using AI?

Reflect the world in your investments

To remain relevant in the future, you may need to overinvest in the people you haven't historically been providing for, appealing to or working with.

Decision 89:
Identify your potential for business development

When identifying new markets, products, services and commercial relationships, look at your existing consumers, audience, or service users, and see if their demographics match those of the entire population.

If you're targeting wealthy customers, do you have Black, disabled, lesbian and young wealthy customers? If you provide a service for low-income workers, do you tailor your support for Chinese, LGBT+ and Dyslexic people? Maybe you target families? Do you reflect single-parent families? Or how about weddings? Do you appeal to same-sex couples or couples with Black or Brown skin? And if people download, stream or interact with your content, who is it that's doing it?

> *Whatever the reason your organisation exists, find out who uses your products or services and who doesn't.*

Whatever the reason your organisation exists, find out who uses your products or services and who doesn't.

Get to know the people you've historically missed out

When you find a gap in your customer base, the next step is to explore how you will appeal to them. You'll need to build trust and credibility to make sure your approach is authentic. People will see straight through being targeted if there's a lack of understanding about who they are, how they live their lives and what's really important to them.

A great way to listen and learn is by partnering with an employee network (Decision 17) who represents the population you'd like to be appealing to. Be open about what you don't know and would like to learn. Suspend your judgement if the feedback is confronting or unfamiliar to your own lived experience. Moments like this can feel like waking up from sleepwalking, before it transforms your thinking and approach.

If you don't have employee networks, you can approach charities and research providers. And if you already use third parties to generate business development ideas, make sure you specify the need for demographic breakdowns when they present findings and recommendations.

Also, make sure you create a deliberately diverse guestlist when you invite customers, consumers or members to participate in feedback panels or events.

Otherwise, feedback will be skewed toward the overrepresented.

Decision 90:
Report on customer experience split by demographic

Whatever you use to track customer experience, break it down by demographic. You can look at things like acquisition, retention, complaints, referrals or satisfaction. Uncovering demographic differences will identify where you could be adding more value.

You'll know what your all-important metrics are. They're likely to be the things you review every month or quarter.

For an example of breaking down reports by demographic see Decision 26.

Decision 91:
Expand your research beyond the 'average' human

One-size-fits-all doesn't work as it's based on designing for an *average* human. I laughed out loud when I read this line in a LinkedIn post – '*An old statistician's joke tells how if you put your feet in the fire and your head in the freezer on average you'll feel fine*'.[14]

There are thousands of examples where one-size-fits-all doesn't work. Take the *racist soap dispenser*[15] that was researched, designed, tested, marketed, manufactured, shipped and installed before a consumer noticed it wouldn't dispense on their Black skin. The sensors only registered pale skin tones. You can find footage on YouTube, and you'll see it only works when the person with Black skin put a white paper towel over their hand. As well as damage to reputation, that's a cost and productivity impact to redevelop the product and replace in all those bathrooms.

Do you remember the urgency to provide personal protective equipment in the Covid-19 global pandemic to keep healthcare workers safe? The template was based on a six-foot man,[16] yet most healthcare workers are women.

I'll bet you've noticed the massive queues for women's toilets in stadiums and theatres when there are rarely queues for the men. That's because the 50/50 allocation doesn't account for half the population needing to sit down to pee, change period products, go more often when pregnant, clean up after flooding during menopause etc.

If you have no physical disabilities, imagine what it's like to travel through a city in a wheelchair, search for step-free access, or reach for lift buttons that have been installed at standing height. And if you're neurotypical, imagine going into a store with music and demonstration videos blaring if you're sensitive to noise. Or, how about discovering a fault in your car's satellite navigation design because the highlighted route isn't colour blind friendly.

The one that gets me most is the disparity in medicine and health outcomes. Patients don't get the right diagnosis or pain treatment because their symptoms don't match the research findings. The trouble here is the participants invited into the research groups weren't always a diverse mix, so the findings and associated recommendations don't apply equally well to everyone.

If something isn't right in your body, and your symptoms are being dismissed as an anomaly, keep pushing.

You'll likely have tons of your own examples of how 'average' doesn't apply to you or others, or you'll be noticing them more and more now. So, I'll stop sharing examples before you feel like it's all hopeless. Because it absolutely isn't.

<u>Involve a diverse mix of people in research and design</u>
It's often impossible to design for every individual. But you can provide for a wider variety of users by involving a diverse mix of people in research and design. Then provide options and evolve as needed.

Getting colleagues involved helps build an inclusive culture and getting customers involved helps create better value and loyalty. Check which user perspectives you're missing, and be intentional about bringing them in.

Decision 92:
Mirror real people in your media and marketing

The messages we consume through the narratives put out into the world through all different types of media can influence how we feel about ourselves and each other. This represents responsibility and opportunity.

Hollywood

The **2019** documentary *'This changes everything'*[17] investigates the underrepresentation and misrepresentation of women in media. Hollywood's leading voices describe *'most of television and film is men making stuff for other men'*. Then men provide most of the ratings, and shows with good ratings influence further investment in similar content. In contrast, women are often hypersexualised, underrepresented and misrepresented with limited character development or opportunity to inspire the audience. I know within three minutes if a woman has been involved in directing, producing, or writing. Because the shows I enjoy have female characters that are perfectly imperfect, funny, stressed, outrageous, intelligent, powerful, deflated and every other character dimension. Just like all the women in my life.

Advertising

In response to the Black Lives Matter movement in **2020** it seemed every advert and magazine cover went from having a cast that was a complete whitewash to a complete blackwash. Or every family was mixed race.

While this wasn't great for authenticity, it demonstrated how easy it is to not mindlessly perpetuate the overrepresentation of certain groups. If only you try.

In **2021**, broadcaster ITV partnered with System1 Group and DECA Diversity Media Consultancy to deliver the research *'Feeling Seen: How diverse advertising unites us'*.[18] They completed over 10,000 interviews with people of the demographic groups featured in each of the adverts they were asked to watch. They found a significant boost in happiness when a group is represented, and that good adverts have something important in common. They feature ordinary people living their ordinary lives. There's a great quote from ITV's Group Director of Diversity and Inclusion, Ade Rawcliffe: *'We are changed by what we see. Just as we are changed when we are seen'*. There was no suggestion of needing to make different adverts for different audiences. Instead, they found the best way to make a great advert is to make a great advert, which is also inclusive. Not to make an inclusive advert and hope it turns out great.

> While this wasn't great for authenticity, it demonstrated how easy it is to not mindlessly perpetuate the overrepresentation of certain groups. If only you try.

Sport

In **2022** the England Lionesses won the women's European Football Championships. It was the first time an England team had raised an international trophy at Wembley Stadium in London since 1966.[19] The audience and sports pundits were all behind the women's team. The 87,192 people who went along to watch became the biggest crowd on record for a Euro's match in women's or men's history. And another 20 million watched from home. It was a wonderful moment of unity and celebration, and you could see just how much it meant to the players and entire coaching team. They made history.

It was also significant because the players were there, not because of the system, but despite the system. Just four years earlier the women's team had been begging to use stadiums to host their games and so many said no, because there was a belief that women didn't play very well or draw a big enough crowd.

Did you know there were women's clubs in the **1890s**?[20] And in **1921** in response to the rising popularity of the women's game and concerns about it eclipsing the men's game, the Football Association (FA) banned women from playing on Football League grounds. The FA said, '*the game of football is quite unsuitable for females and ought not to be encouraged*'. Now obviously, lots has changed since then. But the fact is, men have kept women behind with less opportunity, investment, sponsorship and media coverage. That's not a level playing field.

Whether you influence screen or print media, one-off events or entire seasons, look at the last 12 months and see who you've been amplifying to determine who else you will amplify from now on.

Decision 93:
Demonstrate your understanding of historical disadvantage

Does your corporate narrative demonstrate you understand EDI? The answer can only be yes when prospective employees and customers, industry, or sector peers etc. can see you're aware of historic disadvantages and how you're working toward providing greater equity in people's lives. Your corporate narrative needs to go beyond an equal opportunity statement and list of initiatives. It needs to describe how you're adapting the work you're known for, to work better for everyone.

> *" Your corporate narrative needs to go beyond an equal opportunity statement and list of initiatives. It needs to describe how you're adapting the work you're known for, to work better for everyone.*

Own the changes you need to make

Getty Images, which holds one of the largest photo collections in the world, spent two years creating *The Black History & Culture Collection*, with 30,000 rarely seen images dating back to the 1800s.[21] The collection is for non-commercial use, to inspire educational projects that build a deeper understanding of Black History that goes beyond enslavement and colonisation.

In response to why they've done this, they say,

> 'Historically, Getty Images and the photography industry have not worked from a foundation of diversity equity and inclusion. For too long, the historically dominant cultural structures that have built the photography industry and archives have been grounded in white supremacy dating back to the 19th Century and beyond. Getty Images is committed to changing that. The Black History and Culture Collection is part of a broader programme of activity that addresses the commitments Getty Images has made toward anti-racism, inclusion, and dismantling discrimination. One of the commitments centres around granting broader access to Getty Images' content for education and reflection on cultural heritage'.

This is a fantastic example of corporate allyship.

Responding to global events

The same goes for how you respond to global events and recognise the impact they have on different communities. Do you use your brand as a force for good? Do you mobilise support behind crisis experts? Do you acknowledge the impact on people? See more in Decision 98.

People want to know more than what you provide. They also want to see you care about humanity. And when your organisation is open to learning and takes action, others can replicate and the whole industry or sector raises their game.

Reflection section

Key decision themes

- Finding out who you historically haven't been appealing to or providing for represents an opportunity for business development.

- Reporting on customer experience will identify where you could be adding more value to some customer groups.

- You don't need to design for every individual scenario.

- The messages we consume through the media can influence how we feel about ourselves and each other, which represents a responsibility and opportunity.

- People want to know you care about humanity.

Questions to answer before we move on

■ Which demographics are your products or services currently appealing to?

■ How do you currently measure customer or service user experience?

■ What opportunities are there to better reflect real people in your media and marketing?

Boost your wider-world impact

Your inclusion vision might start off focused on employees and customers, but as confidence grows, your commitment can extend much further. And the greatest social and environmental impact your organisation makes will be the result of specific decisions and investments.

In an HBR article on sustainability the authors guide companies to embrace the synergies between profit and societal benefits.[22] They share an example of a joint venture called BoKlok, between construction company Skanska and home furnishing company IKEA.

The objective was to develop energy-efficient housing that teachers, nurses and other lower-wage workers can afford to buy or rent. To set maximum sale prices they use analysis of salaries, cost of living and typical monthly expenses.

BoKlok manufacture homes in a factory which reduces both the cost and carbon emissions produced during construction. And since 2010 they've built 14,000 affordable homes while routinely outperforming Skanska's conventional construction business.

A great example of thinking about people + planet + profit.

Decision 94:
Connect colleagues working on inclusion and sustainability

Every day decisions made in every organisation impact both people and planet. Be it where you buy goods or services from, paying wages or salaries that meet the cost of living, or reducing your carbon emissions. So, it makes sense to consider your Inclusion Vision and your Environmental, Social and Governance (ESG) Vision alongside each other.

Tools to guide you
The United Nations' 17 Sustainable Development Goals provide a blueprint to achieve a more sustainable future, by representing a call to action for all countries to promote prosperity and protect the planet.[23]

There are tons of ESG experts out there and it's another growing skill set much like EDI. If you're not sure where to start, check out B Corp. It's a growing global movement to certify for-profit organisations for their social and environmental performance.[24] And the non-profit network is aiming to transform the global economy by assessing the impact of its member organisations. More than 150,000 businesses are using their free-to-use digital tool to measure, manage and improve positive impact performance for environment, communities, customers, suppliers, employees and shareholders.[25] It really gets you thinking.

Whether your ESG agenda is focused on oceans being plastic free, eradicating animal cruelty in household products, providing financial education to reduce poverty or something else, they all have something in common. Human beings are involved, and they're focused on making things better for future generations.

Chances are, you've got different people in different departments guiding the organisation on inclusion and sustainability, and frankly, it's big and overwhelming work. No one person will have all the answers so find the opportunities to bring them together, mirror messaging and the work itself where it makes sense. They're guaranteed to learn something from each other, and it'll make their independent work better.

Decision 95:
Move to ethical pension plans

Whether it's going vegan or using their cars less, many of your employees are making small changes to their daily lives to reduce harm to the planet. A significant way to support them is to provide sustainable pensions which invest in organisations focused on the issues they care about, such as climate change, gender equality or human rights.

Research indicates that moving a £100,000 pension pot with a traditional portfolio including oil and gas companies to a *positive impact portfolio* is the equivalent of taking five or six cars off the road a year.[26]

The growth of funds invested along ESG principles has been rapid in recent years, with global ESG-linked funds taking in nearly $350 billion in 2020 compared with $165 billion in 2019. The trend is being driven by investors wanting to align money with values and the model is shifting away from '*screening out*' specific stocks to '*screening in*' stocks for companies that are making positive changes to society and the environment.

If 10% of employees in every organisation did that, the global impact on making the world a better place for everyone would be huge!

Decision 96:
Diversify your supply chain

Depending on the size of your operation, your supply chain could have tens, thousands, or millions of people contributing to delivering your purpose. And it's becoming the norm for organisations to review who you get goods and services from, so you can choose suppliers who share your values and avoid those who don't. The decisions you make about your suppliers can either have a hugely negative impact on the world or a hugely positive one.

Ethical sourcing
Ethical souring is an approach to accounting for the impacts on people and communities when finding products and services. Let's take something widely available where ethical sourcing isn't yet a consistent reality – clothing.

According to Business Insider, fashion production produces 10% of total global carbon emissions.[27] It also dries up water sources and pollutes rivers and streams. What's more, 85% of all textiles go to the dump each year! Clothing production has roughly doubled since 2000, and even washing clothes releases 500,000 tons of microfibres into the ocean each year, which is the equivalent of 50 billion plastic bottles. According to the UN Framework Convention on Climate Change, emissions from textile manufacturing alone are projected to skyrocket by more than 60% by 2030.[28]

'*Fast fashion*' is loud in conversations about environmental sustainability, as cheaply produced garments that copy latest catwalk styles are quickly provided to stores to maximise sales on current trends. Pollution statistics suggest polyester (material derived from a chemical reaction involving petroleum, air and water) is quickly becoming the go-to material. It's cheaper and easier to work with, but the production of just one polyester T-shirt results in 262% more CO_2 emissions than a cotton T-shirt![29]

The '*Tailored Wages 2019: The state of pay in the global garment industry*' report analysed responses from 20 top clothing brands. It found none of the workers they pay to make their clothing in Asia, Africa, Central America or Eastern Europe are paid enough to escape the poverty trap.[30]

This is hardly ethical sourcing.

Inclusive Procurement Model

HS2 is Britain's high-speed rail line being built to connect London with the northeast, and back in 2019 I heard the Head of EDI for HS2 share their Inclusive Procurement Model at *'The Race at Work Summit'*.

At the peak of construction over 34,000 people will be needed.[31] With 60% of employment being subcontracted, they recognised they'd need companies of all shapes and sizes, from small to medium-sized enterprises with a few employees, to giant multinationals. So, they built inclusion into their procurement decisions, firmly stating that organisations with an EDI plan that was reviewed and improved regularly could make the difference between winning a contract or not.[32] They also stated expectations for larger companies to deliver more and lead the way in supporting smaller organisations. In a three-year period, they reported spending £30 billion in Black, Asian and minority ethnic owned businesses.

Here we see the huge impact an organisation can have when they choose to be conscious about their supply chain.

Tender process

Is your tender process for new suppliers inclusive? If the same process designed for large business is applied to small and medium businesses, the answer is no.

Here are the steps of a typical scenario:

1. The organisation prepares a detailed *'Request for Information'* (RFI) or *'Invitation to Tender'* (ITT) document.
2. They share the document with suppliers they're interested in working with.
3. Interested suppliers dedicate time to read, research and reflect, then submit a response.
4. Shortlisted suppliers attend a pitch and Q&A session.
5. A supplier is selected.

Your intention is likely to run a fair and transparent process, but that's not how it's working in practice. Responding to an RFI or ITT is labour intensive. It's typically several days' work and creates a disproportionate disadvantage for small and medium-sized organisations who don't have the resources to employ people to work on tenders. And when seeking consultancy rather than a product, it's essentially seeking expertise and knowledge without paying for it!

The worst impact is for solo business owners, as 100% of time spent on responding to RFIs is 100% of time spent not earning. So, many decline the invitation. And because so many solo-owned businesses are owned by women and minorities, your organisation is limiting the opportunity to work with these groups. You could be missing the benefit of working with people with a broader range of expertise than that held by your existing catalogue of suppliers, who may all share similar business and life experiences.

You may need to experiment to find the right approach and here are a few ideas:

- Invite suppliers to a 30-minute briefing call (instead of sending out multi-page documents) and ask them to submit a proposal in their own format.
- Design bespoke processes for different-sized suppliers.
- Pay small suppliers for time spent working through your procurement process.

T&Cs

Here you need to consider the admin burden of issuing every supplier no matter their size the same set of terms and conditions (T&Cs). If only five of the clauses apply, resist sending out every possible clause that every possible supplier may need to be aware of. It's a burden felt disproportionately by small suppliers. You should also remove any indemnities and clauses that make it impossible for small businesses to bid or compete.

Payment terms

Your payment terms should consider the cashflow implications for the varying sizes of organisations in your supply chain. They'll need to pay their own employees, suppliers, expenses etc., and the recommendation is a maximum of 30 days. In 2021, the UK government announced a *Prompt Payment Code* to encourage larger companies to stand by smaller suppliers and protect jobs and growth as we build back after the Covid-19 pandemic.[33]

The worst payment terms I've seen is an organisation with an annual turnover of £390 million wanting to pay small businesses '*end of month plus 90 days*' after invoice. That's over a quarter of a year! It lacks economic responsibility.

Communications

Another small but important point is to be gender inclusive in your communications. Switch '*Dear Sir/ Madam*' with '*Dear Supplier*'.

Decision 97: Report on supplier diversity

At least once a year, you should review the diversity of your supply chain and preferred suppliers to see what percentage of your purchases are from companies that are majority-owned or led by women or people from underrepresented groups.

With that information, you can update your procurement process to highlight any over- and underrepresentation. Then build an *inclusion reminder* (Decision 11) into the procurement process guidance for reviewing the supply chain, inviting organisations to tender and making final decisions.

Your approach will need to consider each country's laws around collecting data (Decision 25), and if you have a large supply chain you're likely to benefit from working with an external body, for example MSDUK or WeConnect International.

Decision 98:
Donate to and organise for those most in need

Many organisations contribute to charities and provide time for colleagues to volunteer. The overall contribution tends to favour organisations people have already heard of. Perhaps the charities and partners you work with have been introduced by one person's personal connection, a quick vote, or multiple people choosing individual causes that matter to them most.

To maximise your opportunity to reach those most in need, I recommend a blend of two approaches:

1. Organisation contributions – allocate a large proportion of your overall company donations to charities serving underrepresented groups in the communities you serve.

2. Individual contributions – provide choice for your employees through time off for volunteering, payroll deductions to charity before tax, or company-matched fundraising schemes for people who've raised money for their chosen cause.

Food banks

Food banks are unfortunately all too common with more and more people pushed into food poverty. Deliveroo, a British online food delivery company, partnered with The Trussell Trust, a food bank charity, to provide up to two million meals and vital support for people facing hardship.[34] Deliveroo customers donate by adding a round-up donation to their in-app food orders. And Deliveroo employees share time, skills and expertise with The Trussell Trust and other local food banks.

What a fantastic example of a brand purpose connecting community, customers and colleagues.

Accommodation for people fleeing war

When seeking safety in another country, refugees often flee war, violence, conflict, or persecution with little more than the clothes on their back. Airbnb operates a global online marketplace, matching hosts with people seeking accommodation, primarily for short-term holiday stays. But in response to the Afghan refugee crisis, Airbnb co-ordinated with hosts to provide refugees with accommodation around the world. The stays are funded by a combination of Airbnb, donations, and hosts providing beds for free or at a discount. Refugees find a place to stay by connecting with one of Airbnb's resettlement agencies or non-profit partners. By February 2022 Airbnb had reached their initial goal of facilitating 20,000 Afghan refugee guests.[35]

A wonderful example of combining organisation purpose with real-world need.

Connecting people across the world
Following the Russian invasion of Ukraine in 2022, millions of people fled their homes, crossing into neighbouring countries including Poland, Hungary and Moldova.

Vodafone, a multinational telecommunications company, has been helping refugees stay in touch with friends and family and keep up to date with latest news. Vodafone has been co-ordinating relief efforts in countries bordering Ukraine with employees volunteering to install free-to-use Instant WiFi and charging points.[36] They've also offered free connectivity to 200,000 refugees arriving in the UK, and their *'Tech Appeal'* has provided 3,000 smartphones and 1,000 portable power banks.

Another example of organisation purpose being a force for good.

From painting fences at a local hospice to providing lifelines for the hungry and homeless, the possibilities for broadening your impact are endless.

Decision 99:
Influence your industry or sector, policy and decision makers

As you deliver your inclusion vision and your confidence grows, share your approach to make your impact even bigger. Get on stage at well-respected events, be open about what you've learnt on social media, collaborate with industry and sector peers for greater social and environmental progress. And work with policy and decision makers to provide a path for less experienced organisations to follow.

When everyone shares what they've learnt, it inspires further progress and the more organisations working to make the world a better place, the better.

Reflection section

Key decision themes

- People working on inclusion and ESG can learn from each other and make their independent work better.

- The pension model is shifting away from *'screening out'* traditional portfolios including oil and gas companies, to *'screening in'* companies making positive changes to society and the environment.

- Your procurement process may not be the *'fair'* selection process you think it is.

- Reporting on supplier diversity will highlight opportunities to work with more organisations owned and led by women and people from underrepresented groups.

- The possibilities to align charitable donations and volunteering with your Inclusion Vision and ESG Vision are endless.

- Sharing your approach and what you've learnt creates a path for other organisations to follow.

Questions to answer before we move on

- Do you provide ethical pension plans?

- Think about the last three suppliers you've worked with – how many of them were owned or led by women or people from underrepresented groups?

- Which events or publications could you aspire to sharing your progress in (if you aren't already)?

Part 7

Your impact on the world

Woo-hoo. You made it to the section where you'll decide what to do. Either that or you jumped straight here for the shortcut, which you're welcome to do in this judgement-free zone.

Can you believe we've covered 99 Decisions for conscious inclusion?! I'm a bit shocked as I had no idea it would be that many when I started writing. Thank you for staying with me.

You'll have noticed that the underlying theme is to move away from one-size-fits-all, and make the work you do work better for everyone.

Let's help you make it stick.

Five simple habits to guide you every day

The work of inclusion isn't always easy as it challenges so much of what we've been taught was the right way to do things. The good news is, it is simple when practised and built into your everyday approach to showing up at work and in life.

I've distilled five habits from years of research to find what really works, and you can consider them your cheat sheet, for every big (and small) decision you make every day. This everyday thinking is your sure-fire way to make sure your organisation remains relevant in the future, and you leave a legacy to be proud of. Whenever I do keynote speaking, this is the moment everyone leans forward.

Staying true to *doing one thing brilliantly*, pick one habit at a time, and practise it until it becomes the usual way you operate. Then come back and pick another.

Habit 1:
Make sure there's a mix

Whenever you're putting a group of people together, make sure there's a diverse mix. Start with the people that come to mind immediately, then take a look to see where you have overrepresentation and extend your invitations to address it.

This applies to meetings, recruitment shortlists, guest speakers, project teams, customer feedback sessions, research groups, product testing, advertising campaigns, gathering feedback... and anything else you can think of.

Habit 2:
Invite everyone to join the conversation

Once you have the mix, invite everyone to join the conversation. This goes back to the party analogy in Part 1. If you've invited people to be there, make sure you value, hear and involve them.

This is how you bring together the knowledge from new hires, long servers, people with different thinking styles and personalities, mixed demographics and cultures etc.

Habit 3:
Deliberately seek alternative perspectives

Go beyond your usual 'go to' people for feedback and advice.

This is a big one for me personally. I was guilty of being in a hurry, going to the people who already knew my work and knew how I liked to receive feedback, and probably only really wanting them to suggest the odd tweak. They all gave me valuable feedback, but they usually shared a similar profile.

When I started deliberately asking people in other teams and with different life experiences, I got much richer feedback, and this habit has made my work better ever since. At the beginning it felt like going slower to go faster, until I realised I was making fewer alterations once I'd gone live with new work.

Habit 4:
Ask what would make people included

This might look like saying, '*Hey Catherine, I noticed you didn't speak up in that meeting and I really value your thinking, is there something I can do differently so you're more comfortable taking part?*'

Notice how the focus is on what you can do, not what Catherine can do. The response might be as simple as letting Catherine know you'd welcome her contribution on [insert subject] ahead of the meeting so she has time to reflect and provide a valuable contribution.

Habit 5:
Get to know people who aren't just like you

Think about the five or six people closest to you in your work or home life. Chances are you have lots in common, as that's how we're socialised and how we form friendships. And that's ok. If that's true for you, next is to recognise how heavily influenced you are by those five or six people. Maybe it's the sports you enjoy, how you vote in political campaigns, your sense of humour etc.

Getting to know people who are not just like you helps you realise you have more in common than you think. It also increases your empathy and improves your awareness when making decisions that might affect them.

There are many ways to do this at work

You can join employee networks representing people with a different demographic profile to you as an ally, then sign up to receive their newsletters and attend the events they host. If there are multiple networks in your organisation, join them all, scan their newsletters and attend at least one event per quarter. Then show your support when you get there.

You can also spend time with other teams and invite a more diverse mix of people to the meetings you host.

Learn more in private

Another way to learn about people who aren't just like you is in private, by consciously curating the media you consume in your everyday life:

- **Look through your social media feeds:** Who do you follow? Whose posts do you interact with?

- **Review your reading collection and podcast library:** Which authors, hosts and guests are you listening to?

- **Increase variety in the TV and movies you watch:** Who are the directors, producers and writers who are entertaining and educating you?

Practise regularly

As you can see, these five habits are super simple and don't take much effort. And with a bit of practice, they'll have a huge impact on broadening your perspective, upping your empathy and helping you be more consciously inclusive.

Create your 12-month roadmap

If you're anything like me, your brain is sparking ideas left right and centre and you just want to get on and make the world a little bit better than you found it. And you're confident that all that thinking will eventually lead you toward the actions that will make the most difference.

You might also be wondering what you'll do when and be feeling slightly overwhelmed. It's ok. I get it.

Let me help you work out your roadmap for the next 12 months. This is the first step in breaking down your big ambition into achievable action. Remember there are no prizes for who does the most, because the ultimate prize is the collective impact of everyone who has read this book doing one thing brilliantly, at a time.

Decision checklist
Here's a list of all the decisions we've covered in the order they're described in the book. I want you to tick off anything that's already happening in your organisation (and do a little happy dance), then highlight anything you can realistically get done in the next 12 months and place a question mark next to anything you need to explore a bit further.

The decision checklist is also available in the workbook you can download at www.compellingculture.co.uk/book

Decisions from Part 3:
How to create an inclusive culture

<u>Build solid foundations</u>
- ☐ 1. Use a model for change
- ☐ 2. Create the belief change is possible
- ☐ 3. Have a plan for not always getting it right
- ☐ 4. Set your inclusion leaders up for success

<u>Lead with courage and vulnerability</u>
- ☐ 5. Dedicate time to learn and share fears
- ☐ 6. Give permission to yourself and others
- ☐ 7. Boost peer-to-peer learning
- ☐ 8. Encourage respectful disagreement

<u>Challenge automatic (biased) thinking</u>
- ☐ 9. Slow down when making big decisions
- ☐ 10. Redefine what a good leader is
- ☐ 11. Build inclusion reminders into routine discussions
- ☐ 12. Build a routine to find out what everyone *really* thinks

<u>Supercharge employee networks</u>
- ☐ 13. Define what a network is (and isn't)
- ☐ 14. Educate as you celebrate notable dates
- ☐ 15. Sponsor network success
- ☐ 16. Get people involved in their own way

☐   17. Encourage collaboration for greater impact
☐   18. Be specific about the *'give and get'*
       exchange

Share the spotlight and unite people
☐   19. Create a stage for the modern age
☐   20. Ask what people need when attending
       events
☐   21. Use language that unites people
☐   22. Make your communications accessible
☐   23. Share talking and listening time in meetings

Decisions from Part 4:
How to embed inclusion into policies and process

Use data to unlock sustainable progress
☐   24. Work with subject matter experts
☐   25. Collect good data and protect it
☐   26. Report on inclusion
☐   27. Report on diversity at every level
☐   28. Report on the recruitment process
☐   29. Report on people process outcomes

Evolve policies to be human centred
☐   30. Go beyond employment law
☐   31. Provide support for Women, Trans and Non-
       Binary people
☐   32. Mirror parental leaves
☐   33. Introduce carers leave
☐   34. Remove length of service restrictions
☐   35. Use gender-neutral language

☐ 36. Demonstrate zero tolerance to harassment and bullying

☐ 37. Avoid the line manager lottery

☐ 38. Make information easy to find and understand

☐ 39. Build based on feedback from your employees

Be flexible and religion friendly

☐ 40. Focus on results delivered instead of hours worked

☐ 41. Move away from the full-time default

☐ 42. Resize workloads

☐ 43. Create options for shift workers

☐ 44. Introduce bank holiday swaps

Shrink pay and benefit gaps

☐ 45. Reframe the focus on pay gaps

☐ 46. Provide financial assistance when needed

☐ 47. Determine your CEO to average worker pay ratio

☐ 48. Pay a <u>real</u> living wage

☐ 49. Monitor independent pay decisions

☐ 50. Provide benefits that match life circumstances

☐ 51. Recognise your rocks and rockstars

☐ 52. Repurpose long-service awards

☐ 53. Reflect people, planet and profit in your bonus structure

Decisions from Part 5:
How to address overrepresentation

Be specific about who you want to attract
- ☐ 54. Focus on building collective intelligence
- ☐ 55. Make work experience affordable for everyone
- ☐ 56. Know the difference between positive discrimination and positive action
- ☐ 57. Set specific targets for each department
- ☐ 58. Invite people to 'try before you apply' experiences
- ☐ 59. Provide consistent guidance for hiring managers

Update your approach to hiring
- ☐ 60. Redesign job adverts
- ☐ 61. Advertise all vacancies
- ☐ 62. Make diverse shortlists standard
- ☐ 63. Restructure your '*Recommend a Friend*' scheme
- ☐ 64. Change the filters in your Applicant Tracking System (ATS)
- ☐ 65. Make sure your ATS is accessible
- ☐ 66. Stop asking for salary history
- ☐ 67. Ask candidates to provide their demographic information
- ☐ 68. Ask candidates if you need to adjust your process
- ☐ 69. Provide interview questions in advance

☐ 70. Have more than one person make hiring
   decisions
☐ 71. Reflect your commitments in your employer
   brand

Be deliberate about career progression
☐ 72. Find out why careers are progressing at
   different rates
☐ 73. Sponsor the people you want to stay
☐ 74. Segment marketing for career development
   programmes
☐ 75. Design 'talent escalators' for internal mobility
☐ 76. Build your reserves bench before you have a
   vacancy

Diversify the Board of Directors
☐ 77. Challenge the status quo for selection criteria
☐ 78. Shift the power dynamic

Decisions from Part 6:
How to operate inclusively

Provide buildings that welcome everyone
☐ 79. Allocate budget for adjustments
☐ 80. Go beyond accessibility audits
☐ 81. Signpost trans-inclusive toilets
☐ 82. Create uninterruptible spaces for faith and
   lactation

Provide friendly technology
- ☐ 83. Make digital services, websites and apps accessible
- ☐ 84. Make internal systems and tools accessible
- ☐ 85. Modernise employee and customer profiles
- ☐ 86. Provide a hardware menu
- ☐ 87. Replace outdated terminology
- ☐ 88. Don't rely on Artificial Intelligence (AI) alone

Reflect the world in your investments
- ☐ 89. Identify your potential for business development
- ☐ 90. Report on customer experience split by demographic
- ☐ 91. Expand your research beyond the 'average' human
- ☐ 92. Mirror real people in media and marketing
- ☐ 93. Demonstrate your understanding of historical disadvantage

Boost your wider-world impact
- ☐ 94. Connect colleagues working in inclusion and sustainability
- ☐ 95. Move to ethical pension plans
- ☐ 96. Diversify your supply chain
- ☐ 97. Report on supplier diversity
- ☐ 98. Donate to and organise for those most in need
- ☐ 99. Influence your industry or sector, policy and decision makers

The ultimate reflection section

Next, reflect on all the notes you've made at the end of the chapters and answer these questions:

- **What has been the most useful part of reading this book?**

- **Picture yourself jumping into a time machine and fast forwarding to a year into the future. When you look back on what you've achieved, what's the <u>one</u> big thing you're most proud of?**

- **Who are the other changemakers in your organisation? How can you collaborate?**

- **What help do you need to create your inclusion strategy?**

- **What's the worst that can happen?**

Be brave

Now you've got your 12-month roadmap, a vision to work towards and permission to be brave.

I encourage you to find others who share your passion for making the world a better place. There are loads of people on this mission and connecting with them will fuel you to go further faster.

Take courage in challenging the status quo and the traditional ways things have been done. And when it feels like the mix of perspectives are too contrasting, find the common ground to bring people together and go from there. *Everyone* wants to be valued, heard and involved.

Do one thing brilliantly at a time, help people understand why it matters and keep going until it sticks. Then move on to the next thing and do that brilliantly. And the next, and the next, and the next...

Remember to go where the energy is and use data and feedback from real humans and their real lives to guide you. Understand you'll get things wrong and encourage people to tell you when that happens. Then apologise, give thanks for the feedback, dust yourself off and keep going.

Build a routine to pause, reflect and celebrate all the tiny wins. It's all of those that add up to big change.

And every 12 months, come back to update your decision checklist. Add in anything new you've discovered will make a difference to making your organisation more inclusive for more people. Then, decide what you'll do for the next 12 months.

Learning how to do conscious inclusion might just be the most important thing you'll ever do.

I can't wait for you to see your impact.

Big love

Lady Catherine x

Learning library

Monthly newsletter

Sign up to the much-loved Crown Jewels and Whoopsie-daisy newsletter from Compelling Culture. Each month, the Crown Jewels highlights great things happening in organisations, and the Whoopsie-daisy walks through one example of where it went wrong and what you can learn.

To sign up, visit www.compellingculture.co.uk/newsletter

Books

Bias

Why I'm no longer speaking to white people about race, by Reni Eddo-Lodge

Invisible women, by Caroline Criado Perez

Quiet, by Susan Cain

Motivating change

Drive, by Daniel Pink

Switch, by Chip Heath and Dan Heath

<u>Lead with courage and vulnerability</u>

Dare to lead, by Brené Brown, also look up her podcast of the same name, and watch her Netflix special – **The Call to Courage**

The coaching habit, by Michael Bungay Stanier

How to be right in a world gone wrong, by James O'Brien

<u>Automatic thinking</u>

Thinking fast and slow, by Daniel Kahneman

Inclusion Nudges, by Tinna C. Nielsen & Lisa Kepinski

<u>Wider-world impact</u>

Uncharted, by Margaret Heffernan

Rebel ideas, by Matthew Syed

Articles

D. Clark and C. Smith, **Help your employees be themselves at work**, Harvard Business Review (2014). Available from https://hbr.org/2014/11/help-your-employees-be-themselves-at-work

V. Hunt, D. Layton and S. Prince, **Why diversity matters,** McKinsey (2015). Available from www.mckinsey.com/capabilities/people-and-organizational-performance/our-insights/why-diversity-matters

D. Rock and H. Grant, **Why diverse teams are smarter,** Harvard Business Review (2016). Available from https://hbr.org/2016/11/why-diverse-teams-are-smarter

F. Dobbin and A. Kalev, **Why diversity programmes fail,** Harvard Business Review (2016). Available from https://hbr.org/2016/07/why-diversity-programs-fail

D. Rock, H. Grant and J. Grey, **Diverse teams feel less comfortable – and that's why they perform better,** Harvard Business Review (2016). Available from https://hbr.org/2016/09/diverse-teams-feel-less-comfortable-and-thats-why-they-perform-better

L. Sherbin and R. Rashid, **Diversity doesn't stick without inclusion,** Harvard Business Review (2017). Available from https://hbr.org/2017/02/diversity-doesnt-stick-without-inclusion

S. Turban, L. Freeman and B. Waber, **A study used sensors to show that men and women are treated differently at work,** Harvard Business Review (2017). Available from https://hbr.org/2017/10/a-study-used-sensors-to-show-that-men-and-women-are-treated-differently-at-work?utm_content=buffer7799a&utm_medium=social&utm_source=linkedin.com&utm_campaign=buffer

Fatherhood Institute, **Cash or carry (2017): Fathers combining work and care in the UK** (2017). Available from www.fatherhoodinstitute.org/2022/contemporary-fathers-in-the-uk/

J. Moore, **Diversity makes companies richer says McKinsey. Activist investors take note,** Independent (2018). Available from www-independent-co-uk.cdn. ampproject.org/c/s/www.independent.co.uk/news/ business/comment/diversity-makes-companies-richer-says-mckinsey-activist-investors-take-note-a8167561. html?amp

Department for Business, Energy & Industrial Strategy and Race Disparity Unit, **Race at work 2018: McGregor-Smith review – one year on,** Gov.uk (2018). Available from www.gov.uk/government/publications/race-at-work-2018-mcgregor-smith-review-one-year-on

Accenture, **Our commitment to inclusion & diversity** (n.d.). Available from www.accenture.com/gb-en/about/inclusion-diversity-index

R. Bastian, **Why we need to stop talking about diversity of thought,** Forbes (2019). Available from www.forbes.com/sites/rebekahbastian/2019/05/13/why-we-need-to-stop-talking-about-diversity-of-thought/?sh=3d2fb07767c3

S. Illing, **How meritocracy harms everyone – even the winners,** Vox (2019). Available from www.vox.com/identities/2019/10/21/20897021/meritocracy-economic-mobility-daniel-markovits

McKinsey & Company, **Diversity wins: How inclusion matters** (2020). Available from www.mckinsey.com/

featured-insights/diversity-and-inclusion/diversity-wins-how-inclusion-matters

T. Chamorro-Premuzic, **Implicit bias training doesn't work,** Bloomberg (2020). Available from www.bloomberg.com/opinion/articles/2020-01-04/implicit-bias-training-isn-t-improving-corporate-diversity?leadSource= uverify%20wall

R.J. Ely and D.A. Thomas, **Getting serious about diversity: Enough already with the business case,** Harvard Business Review (2020). Available from https://hbr.org/2020/11/getting-serious-about-diversity-enough-already-with-the-business-case

T. Chamorro-Premuzic, **How valid are the arguments against affirmative action?,** Forbes (2021). Available from www.forbes.com/sites/tomaspremuzic/2021/04/05/how-valid-are-the-arguments-against-affirmative-action/?sh=3d698d294aca

K. Greene, **Dear CEOs: A Gen Zer's open letter to his future employers,** Harvard Business Review (2021). Available from https://hbr.org/2021/06/dear-ceos-a-gen-zers-open-letter-to-his-future-employers

R. Tulshyan and J.-A. Burey, **Stop telling women they have imposter syndrome,** Harvard Business Review (2021). Available from https://hbr.org/2021/02/stop-telling-women-they-have-imposter-syndrome

H. Grant and T. Goldhamer, **Our brains were not built for this much uncertainty,** Harvard Business Review (2021). Available from https://hbr.org/2021/09/our-brains-were-not-built-for-this-much-uncertainty?

M. Sigelman and J.C. Taylor. Jr., **To build a diverse company for the long term, develop junior talent,** Harvard Business Review (2021). Available from https://hbr.org/2021/04/to-build-a-diverse-company-for-the-long-term-develop-junior-talent

YouTube videos

<u>Culture</u>
TV2Play, **TV2: All that we share,** YouTube (n.d.). Available from www.youtube.com/watch?v=jD8tjhVO1Tc

Aligator, **This new Heineken ad is brilliant,** YouTube (n.d.). Available from www.youtube.com/watch?v=et-Iqln7vT4w

LifeAtSky, **Step up, speak up: National Inclusion Week 2019,** YouTube (2019). Available from www.youtube.com/watch?v=_p-t1oNbgA8

<u>Social mobility</u>
Peter D, **Social inequalities explained in a $100 race,** YouTube (n.d.). Available from www.youtube.com/watch?v=4K5fbQ1-zps&t=58s

Intersectionality
Soyheat, **Kids explain intersectionality,** YouTube (n.d.). Available from www.youtube.com/watch?v=WzbADY-CmTs

Disability
Scope, **Four awkward things to avoid saying when you meet a disabled person**, YouTube (n.d.). Available from www.youtube.com/watch?v=y90fEid9akg

How to ADHD, **What exactly is neurodiversity?**, YouTube (n.d.). Available from https://www.youtube.com/watch?v=ALJ3CFRRZpo

LGBT+
Vodafone Group, **Vodafone: Equal at work**, YouTube (n.d.). Available from www.youtube.com/watch?v=4Bv7FuOS5-A

Ad Council, **Love has no labels**, YouTube (n.d.). Available from www.youtube.com/watch?v=PnDgZuGlhHs

BBC Three, **Things not to say to a non-binary person**, YouTube (n.d.). Available from www.youtube.com/watch?v=8b4MZjMVgdk (also lots of other great content under 'things not to say')

Race
chel.by.the.seas, **Jane Elliott "Blue Eyes – Brown Eyes" experiment anti-racism**, YouTube (n.d.). Available from www.youtube.com/watch?v=dLAi78hluFc

yuugo, **Muhammad Ali talks about him growing up confused as to why everything was so "white"**, YouTube (n.d.). Available from www.youtube.com/watch?v=RI6X386Ic9A

Futureism, **This 'Racist soap dispenser' at Facebook office does not work for black people**, YouTube (n.d.). Available from www.youtube.com/watch?v=YJjv_OeiHmo

Jubilee, **Dear child – when black parents have to give "the talk"**, YouTube (n.d.). Available from www.youtube.com/watch?v=Mkw1CetjWwl

Fanpage.it, **Doll test – The effects of racism on children**, YouTube (n.d.). Available from www.youtube.com/watch?app=desktop&v=QRZPw-9sJtQ

Gender

MullenLowe Group, **Inspiring the future – redraw the balance**, YouTube (n.d.). Available from www.youtube.com/watch?v=qv8VZVP5csA&t=2s

B.M. Anderson, **Pixar's new short film examines workplace diversity with humor, insight and a lively ball of yarn**, LinkedIn (2019). Available from https://www.youtube.com/watch?v=B6uuIHpFkuo

crazy videos, **If men breastfed hahahahah**, YouTube (n.d.). Available from www.youtube.com/watch?v=y1j0nv9Jc6o

Viral MEDIA, **Wreck It Ralph 2 'She's a princess' full scene (2018)**, YouTube (n.d.). Available from www.youtube.com/watch?v=-nnbll1LDCg

Girls. Girls. Girls. Magazine, **Be a lady they said**, YouTube (n.d.). Available from www.youtube.com/watch?v=z8ZSDS7zVdU&t=86s

Feminist Frequency, **The Bechdel test for women in movies**, YouTube (n.d.). Available from www.youtube.com/watch?v=bLF6sAAMb4s

Notes

Part 1

[1] F. Daniel, *Equity vs. equality*, Better Bike Share Partnership (2019). Available from https://betterbikeshare. org/2019/10/24/equity-vs-equality/

[2] Britannica, *Industrial revolution* (2022). Available from www.britannica.com/event/Industrial-Revolution#ref347982

[3] UK Parliament, *Equal Franchise Act 1928* (2022). Available from www.parliament.uk/about/living-heritage/ transformingsociety/electionsvoting/womenvote/overview/ thevote/#:~:text=Equal%20Franchise%20Act%201928,to%20 vote%20to%2015%20million

[4] S. Son, *The origin of the 8 hour work day – and why it no longer matters*, TINYpulse by Limeade (2017). Available from www.tinypulse.com/blog/the-origin-of-the-8-hour- work-day-and-why-it-no-longer-matters

[5] Stonewall, *Key dates for lesbian, gay, bi and trans equality* (2016). Available from www.stonewall.org.uk/key-dates- lesbian-gay-bi-and-trans-equality

[6] Office for National Statistics, *Ethnicity and national identity in England and Wales: 2021* (n.d.). Available from https://www.ons.gov.uk/ peoplepopulationandcommunity/culturalidentity/ethnicity/ bulletins/ethnicgroupenglandandwales/census2021

[7] Disability Equality North West. *Disabled people's movement – history timeline* (n.d.). Available from http://disability-equality.org.uk/history/

[8] The University of Edinburgh. *Support for neurodiversity* (n.d.). Available from www.ed.ac.uk/equality-diversity/disabled-staff-support/neurodiversity-support#:~:text=Most%20people%20are%20neurotypical%2C%20meaning,learns%20and%20processes%20information%20differently

[9] The Crown Publishing Group. *QUIET, by Susan Cain* (n.d.). Available from https://crownpublishing.com/archives/feature/quiet-susan-cain

[10] S. Illing. *How meritocracy harms everyone – even the winners* (2019). Vox. Available from www.vox.com/identities/2019/10/21/20897021/meritocracy-economic-mobility-daniel-markovits

[11] Inclusive Companies. *Sky* (n.d.). Available from www.inclusivecompanies.co.uk/2019casestudies/sky/

Part 2

[1] F. Dobbin and A. Kalev, *Why diversity programs fail*. Harvard Business Review (2016). Available from https://hbr.org/2016/07/why-diversity-programs-fail

[2] H. Wasif, *People from ethnic minorities are changing their names to get a job – I was very nearly one of them*. Inews (2022). Available from https://inews.co.uk/opinion/failed-applications-nearly-changed-name-get-job-1617614

[3] Centre for Social Investigation, Nuffield College, Oxford, *New CSI research reveals high levels of job discrimination faced by ethnic minorities in Britain* (2019). Available from http://csi.nuff.ox.ac.uk/?p=1299

[4] S. Turban, L. Freeman and B. Waber, *A study used sensors to show that men and women are treated differently at work*, Harvard Business Review (2017). Available from https://hbr.org/2017/10/a-study-used-sensors-to-show-that-men-and-women-are-treated-differently-at-work?utm_medium=social&utm_campaign=hbr&utm_source=LinkedIn&tpcc=orgsocial_edit

Part 3

[1] M. Bayoumi, *They are 'civilised' and 'look like us': the racist coverage of Ukraine*, The Guardian (2022). Available from www.theguardian.com/commentisfree/2022/mar/02/civilised-european-look-like-us-racist-coverage-ukraine

[2] M. Ryder, *An open letter on the reporting of Ukraine: Do not let diversity be a casualty of war*, LinkedIn (2022). Available from www.linkedin.com/pulse/open-letter-reporting-ukraine-do-let-diversity-war-marcus-ryder-mbe/?trackingId=OeuqzESfSUaxau91BDwEOQ%3D%3D

[3] M. Michel, *Cultural erasure of women: How women are remembered in history*, Polemics (2021). Available from www.polemics-magazine.com/opinion/cultural-erasure-of-women-how-women-are-remembered-in-history

[4] Monzo, *Our tone of voice* (n.d.). Available from https://monzo.com/tone-of-voice/

Part 4

1 Department for Work and Pensions, *Disability Confident employer scheme*, Gov.uk (2021). Available from www.gov.uk/government/collections/disability-confident-campaign

2 Inclusive Companies, *Inclusive top 50 UK employers* (n.d.). Available from www.inclusivecompanies.co.uk/inclusivetop50/

3 M. Garner, *Dads demand more paternity leave*, Workingmums (2022). Available from www.workingmums.co.uk/dads-demand-more-paternity-leave/

4 Gov.uk, *Shared parental leave and pay* (n.d.). Available from www.gov.uk/shared-parental-leave-and-pay

5 Spotify HR Blog, *Our parental leave 'baby' – now on solids* (2016). Available from https://hrblog.spotify.com/2016/06/21/what-is-wrong-with-spotifys-paid-parental-leave-policy/

6 Carers UK, *Why we're here* (n.d.). Available from www.carersuk.org/about-us/why-we-re-here

7 K. Scott, *Aviva introduces cancer support service for 16,000 UK staff*, Employee Benefits (2017). Available from https://employeebenefits.co.uk/aviva-introduces

8 Bupa UK, *Everybody health; inclusivity in the workplace*, YouTube (n.d.). Available from www.youtube.com/watch?v=69O8EnycZLU

9 Z. Ettinger and F. Olito, *35 vintage photos show what life was like for women 100 years ago*, Insider (2021). Available

from www.insider.com/photos-show-life-like-women-100-years-ago

[10] C. Johnson and A. Moore, *Zurich sees leap in women applying for senior roles after offering all jobs as flexible*, Zurich (2020). Available from www.zurich.co.uk/media-centre/zurich-sees-leap-in-women-applying-for-senior-roles-after-offering-all-jobs-as-flexible

[11] Share My Telly Job, *Our mission* (n.d.). Available from www.sharemytellyjob.com/our-mission/

[12] S. Forsdick, *Meet the company letting staff 'pick and mix' their bank holidays*, Raconteur (2022). Available from www.raconteur.net/hr/company-staff-choose-bank-holidays/

[3] Imran Sama, *Imran Sama's post*, LinkedIn (n.d.). Available from www.linkedin.com/posts/imran-sama-357987162_sky-diversityinclusion-ramadan2020-activity-6665757092193931265-ClJl?utm_source=share&utm_medium=member_desktop

[14] Government Equalities Office, *Gender pay gap reporting: guidance for employers*, Gov.uk (2022). Available from www.gov.uk/government/collections/gender-pay-gap-reporting

[15] B. Francis-Devine and L. Booth, *The gender pay gap*, House of Commons (2022). Available from https://commonslibrary.parliament.uk/research-briefings/sn07068/

[16] M. Race, *Inflation drives fastest fall in real pay on record*, BBC News (2022). Available from www.bbc.co.uk/news/business-62550069

[17] L. Howard, *Cost of living crisis: Boosted winter fuel payments roll out to 11.6 million pensioners*, Forbes (2022). Available from www.forbes.com/uk/advisor/energy/cost-of-living-crisis/

[18] John Lewis Partnership, *Half-year results 22/23* (2022). Available from www.johnlewispartnership.co.uk/media/press/y2022/John-Lewis-Partnership-unaudited-interim-results-for-the-26-weeks-ended-30-July-2022.html

[19] BBC News, *Super-rich increase their share of world's income* (2021). Available from www.bbc.co.uk/news/business-59565690

[20] Economic Policy Institute, *CEO pay soared nearly 19% in 2020* (2021). Available from www.epi.org/press/ceo-pay-soared-nearly-19-in-2020-ceos-made-351-times-as-much-as-the-typical-worker/

[21] Joost, *The idea CEO-to-employee pay ratio? Much lower than you think*, Corporate Rebels (n.d.). Available from https://corporate-rebels.com/ideal-ceo-to-employee-pay-ratio/

[22] CBS News, *CEO on why giving all employees minimum salary of $70,000 still 'works' six years later: 'Our turnover rate was cut in half'* (2021). Available from www.cbsnews.com/news/dan-price-gravity-payments-ceo-70000-employee-minimum-wage/

[23] Living Wage Foundation, *Become a living wage employer* (n.d.). Available from www.livingwage.org.uk/become-a-living-wage-employer

Part 5

[1] Peter D., *Social inequalities explained in a $100 race*, YouTube (n.d.). Available from www.youtube.com/ watch?v=4K5fbQ1-zps

[2] WarnerMedia, *Equity & inclusion report* (2020/2021). Available from www.warnermedia.com/gb/equity-inclusion-report

[3] Ofcom, *Report: Equity, diversity and inclusion in TV and radio* (2022). Available from www.ofcom.org.uk/tv-radio-and-on-demand/information-for-industry/guidance/diversity/diversity-equal-opportunities-tv-and-radio

[4] Sky, *Get into tech* (n.d.). Available from http:// getintotech.sky.com/

[5] Sky, *Trainee Home Service Engineer Programme* (n.d.). Available from https://careers.sky.com/women-in-home-service/

[6] Sky, *Early careers* (n.d.). Available from https://careers.sky. com/earlycareers/

[7] Harvard Business Review, *Tap the talent your hiring algorithms are missing* (2022). Available from https://hbr. org/2022/05/tap-the-talent-your-hiring-algorithms-are-missing

[8] Unlock, *Ban the box* (n.d.). Available from https://unlock. org.uk/project/ban-the-box/

[9] Recruit!, *Principles of fair chance recruitment* (n.d.). Available from http://recruit.unlock.org.uk/fair-chance-recruitment/principles/#read-more-about-principle-1

[10] Zurich, *How will Gen Z change the workplace?* (2022). Available from www.zurich.com/en/media/magazine/2022/how-will-gen-z-change-the-future-of-work

[11] K. Greene, *Dear CEOs: A Gen Zer's open letter to his future employers* (2021). Harvard Business Review (2021). Available from https://hbr.org/2021/06/dear-ceos-a-gen-zers-open-letter-to-his-future-employers

[12] V. Myers, *Our progress on inclusion: 2021 update*, Netflix (2022). Available from https://about.netflix.com/en/news/our-progress-on-inclusion-2021-update

[13] A. Cohen, *What is a 'Peter problem'? Jaw dropping study of U.K. CEOs reveals more named Peter than women*, Fast Company (2020). Available from www.fastcompany.com/90534066/what-is-a-peter-problem-jaw-dropping-study-of-u-k-ceos-reveals-more-named-peter-than-women#:~:text=Which%20brings%20us%20to%20the,of%20the%20population%20is%20female

[14] The Parker Review Committee, *Improving the ethnic diversity of UK boards*, EY (2022). Available from https://assets.ey.com/content/dam/ey-sites/ey-com/en_uk/topics/diversity/ey-what-the-parker-review-tells-us-about-boardroom-diversity.pdf

[15] www.principality.co.uk/en/about-us/Latest/20220613-Principality-creates-associate-board-roles-to-support-development-of-future-directors

[16] N. Kumleben, *Europe's super league is dead, but UEFA needs reform*, Foreign Policy (2021). Available from https://foreignpolicy.com/2021/07/18/soccer-football-uefa-europe-super-league-champions-euros-

reform/#:~:text=The%20plan%20quickly%20collapsed%20
after,for%20the%20league%20in%20perpetuity

[17] Liverpool FC, *LFC launches Supporters Board* (2021).
Available from www.liverpoolfc.com/news/lfc-launches-
supporters-board

[18] Liverpool Supporters' Union – Spirit of Shankly, *About us*
(n.d.). Available from https://spiritofshankly.com/about/

Part 6

[1] The National Archives, *Equality Act 2010*, Legislation.
gov.uk (n.d.). Available from www.legislation.gov.uk/
ukpga/2010/15/contents

[2] Crazy Videos, *If men breastfed*, YouTube (n.d.). Available
from www.youtube.com/watch?v=y1j0nv9Jc6o

[3] W3C, *How to meet WCAG (quick reference)*
(2019). Available from www.w3.org/WAI/WCAG21/
quickref/?showtechniques=136

[4] Gov.uk, *Understanding WCAG 2.1* (n.d.). Available from
www.gov.uk/service-manual/helping-people-to-use-your-
service/understanding-wcag

[4] J. Jones, *151 years of progress: A timeline of women's
rights and gender equality in the UK*, Yahoo!life (2017).
Available from https://uk.style.yahoo.com/151-years-of-
progress-a-timeline-of-womens-rights-and-gender-equality-
in-the-uk-123243878.html

[5] Government of Singapore Land Transport Authority, *Green
Man+* (n.d.). Available from www.lta.gov.sg/content/

ltagov/en/getting_around/driving_in_singapore/intelligent_
transport_systems/green_man.html

[6] F. Biles, *Is your tech language racist?*, Lloyds Banking
Group (2021). Available from www.lloydsbankinggroup.
com/insights/is-your-tech-language-racist.html

[7] R. Woodgate, *How to check for inclusive language in
Microsoft Word*, How-to Geek (2020). Available from www.
howtogeek.com/677694/how-to-check-for-inclusive-
language-in-microsoft-word/

[8] J. Schmich and S. Mohs, *How a bot changed the way we
talk with each other*, Medium (2021). Available from https://
medium.com/geekculture/how-a-bot-changed-the-way-
we-talk-with-each-other-aea92064da2e

[9] Slack, *Inclusive bot* (n.d.). Available from https://slack.
com/apps/A034T9X5YAU-inclusive-bot?tab=more_info

[10] Inclusive Bot (n.d.). Available from https://inclusivebot.
com/#pricing

[11] T. Thomas, *Uber Eats treats drivers as 'numbers not
humans', says dismissed UK courier*, The Guardian (2022).
Available from www.theguardian.com/technology/2022/
jul/27/uber-eats-treats-drivers-as-numbers-not-humans-says-
dismissed-courier

[12] C. Vallance, *Legal action over alleged Uber facial
verification bias*, BBC News (2021). Available from www.
bbc.co.uk/news/technology-58831373

[13] J. Dastin, *Amazon scraps secret AI recruiting tool that
showed bias against women*, Reuters (2018). Available
from www.reuters.com/article/us-amazon-com-jobs-

automation-insight/amazon-scraps-secret-ai-recruiting-tool-that-showed-bias-against-women-idUSKCN1MK08G

14 P. Bosher, *Average is the enemy...* LinkedIn. Available from www.linkedin.com/pulse/average-enemy-paul-bosher/?trackingId=MXDNSX0OO6ym1kdITBI57w%3D%3D

15 Futureism, *This 'Racist soap dispenser' at Facebook office does not work for black people*, YouTube (n.d.). Available from www.youtube.com/watch?v=YJjv_OeiHmo

16 A. Topping, *Sexism on the Covid-19 frontline: 'PPE is made for a 6ft 3in rugby player'*, The Guardian (2020). Available from www.theguardian.com/world/2020/apr/24/sexism-on-the-covid-19-frontline-ppe-is-made-for-a-6ft-3in-rugby-player

17 Popcorn Entertainment, *This changes everything (2019) official trailer*, YouTube (n.d.). Available from www.youtube.com/watch?v=wQoQqpztdIo

18 ITV Media, *Feeling Seen: How diverse advertising unites us* (n.d.). Available from www.itvmedia.co.uk/itv-backing-business/feeling-seen-how-diverse-advertising-unites-us

19 ITV News, *Lionesses make history with Euro 2022 victory beating Germany 2–1* (2022). Available from www.itv.com/news/2022-07-31/england-win-the-uefa-womens-euros-after-beating-germany-2-1

20 The FA, *The history of women's football in England* (n.d.). Available from www.thefa.com/womens-girls-football/history

21 Getty Images (n.d.). Available from www.gettyimages.co.uk/corporate-responsibility/en/bhcc

[22] M.R. Kramer and M.W. Pfitzer, *The essential link between ESG targets and financial performance*, Harvard Business Review (2022). Available from https://hbr.org/2022/09/the-essential-link-between-esg-targets-financial-performance

[23] United Nations, *Take action for the Sustainable Development Goals* (n.d.). Available from www.un.org/sustainabledevelopment/sustainable-development-goals/

[24] B Lab. *Building the movement* (n.d.). Available from www.bcorporation.net/en-us/movement

[25] B Lab. *B impact assessment* (n.d.). Available from www.bcorporation.net/en-us/programs-and-tools/b-impact-assessment

[26] J. Cumbo, *How green is your pension?*, Financial Times (2021). Available from www.ft.com/greenpensions

[27] M. McFall-Johnsen, *The fashion industry emits more carbon than international flights and maritime shipping combined. Here are the biggest ways it impacts the planet*, Business Insider (2019). Available from www.businessinsider.com/fast-fashion-environmental-impact-pollution-emissions-waste-water-2019-10?r=US&IR=T

[28] United Nations Climate Change, *Fashion industry, UN pursue climate action for sustainable development* (2018). Available from https://unfccc.int/news/fashion-industry-un-pursue-climate-action-for-sustainable-development

[29] D. Radonic, *27 revealing fast fashion statistics you need to know in 2022*, FashionDiscounts (2022). Available from https://fashiondiscounts.uk/fast-fashion-statistics/#:~:text=Fast%20fashion%20pollution%20statistics%20suggest,to%20material%20in%20fast%20fashion

[30] Clean Clothes Campaign, *Tailored Wages 2019: The state of pay in the global garment industry* (n.d.). Available from https://cleanclothes.org/file-repository/tailoredwages-fp.pdf/view

[31] HS2, *Building skills to deliver HS2* (n.d.). Available from www.hs2.org.uk/jobs-and-skills/building-skills-to-deliver-hs2/

[32] BERT Animation, *Equity, diversity & inclusion*, YouTube (n.d.). Available from www.youtube.com/watch?v=8TyAIAx_s24

[33] Gov.uk, *Government tackles late payments to small firms to protect jobs* (n.d.). Available from www.gov.uk/government/news/government-tackles-late-payments-to-small-firms-to-protect-jobs

[34] The Trussell Trust, *Deliveroo* (n.d.). Available from www.trusselltrust.org/get-involved/partner-with-us/strategic-partners/deliveroo/

[35] Airbnb, *In times of crisis, be a Host* (n.d.). Available from www.airbnb.org/refugees

[36] M. Wall, *How Vodafone volunteers are helping Ukrainian refugees*, Vodafone (2022). Available from www.vodafone.co.uk/newscentre/news/how-vodafone-volunteers-are-helping-ukrainian-refugees/

Acknowledgements

Lou **Johnson** for being an absolute rockstar chief editing queen! For every red pen mark on the first edit, confidence boost, and SOS call. You were right behind me when I decided to restructure the entire book, and every time I was overthinking a couple of words or sentences. You helped me lift 50,000 words off the page more easily and made writing this book feel like fun. Love you long time.

Every BETA draft reader. It's a big ask to read through a 256-page word document and give feedback. Most of you offered to read a least one chapter, many of you ended up reading the whole thing, and all of you helped me see alternative perspectives. I will forever remember your generosity, encouragement and support. A huge thanks to **Camilla-Astrid Robinson, Daniel Priest, Darren Towers, Ian Santry, Jo Rackham, Kaammini Chanrai, Lorna Kerr, Lou Harvey, Louise Poole, Mark Allan, Mark Ealing, Martha Jennings, Paul Jennings** and **Renee Hunt.**

The Catherine shaped cheer squad. You cheered me on from near and far, never doubted my ability to get it written, and were always keen to hear how it was going. It meant heaps. Thanks also to **BPE Search, Casey Miles, Carlton Netball Club, Sam Giblin, Sam Thompson** and the much cherished **Gold family.**

My family for gracing me the space to write as we lived through Dad's illness and said our goodbyes.

Ritu Mohanka and **Haider Imam** telling me I MUST write this book, **Lucy Adams** for agreeing and introducing me to Alison Jones at Practical Inspiration Publishing. Then **Dr Debra Ramsay** and **Lucien Bowater** for helping me edit the proposal to boost the chances of Alison saying yes!

Alison Jones (for her immediate yes) and the **whole Practical Inspiration Publishing team and their partners** for helping me create a book that looks and feels like me, with the inspiration and guidance I needed along the way.

And finally, thanks to everyone who wrote words of praise for *Conscious Inclusion* and gave the validation I hadn't realised I needed. You rock!

Proud of me.

Grateful to all of you.

About the author

Catherine is straight talking, full of energy and empowers people already passionate about what they do. Having collaborated with executive teams, people across every business area and HR, she understands the complexity in embedding sustainable change. She's been on the inside, knows how organisations operate, and has learnt tons about what works (and what doesn't).

Catherine believes that when employees can be themselves and influence how things are done, not only are their lives improved, they're also more creative and better problem solvers. And when consumers are authentically represented in media, products and services, and in organisations, then communities thrive.

Her superpower is absorbing an organisation's ambition and co-creating a compelling plan everyone can get behind using data to embed change and track progress in every team.

Here's what leaders say they value most from working with her:

Your ability to turn ambition into strategy, strategy into action, and action into results. If I chose one

word, it would be 'outcomes', it's what you're so good at.
Sky

Catherine combines expertise, passion and empathy, and I wouldn't hesitate to recommend her as a partner in EDI or culture work.
dentsu

You always say baby steps and that has been the case. We're making real progress, and that's down to your pragmatic way of taking us through the process.
Principality Building Society

Catherine's counsel will lead you to a place where your organisation is making a better impact on the world. Her insight and sense for what should change is strong, challenging and reassuring.
Bupa

If you're interested in having Catherine help embed conscious inclusion into your organisation, or you'd like to invite her to speak at your next event, visit www.compellingculture.co.uk

Index